INTO THE ASH

An Apocalyptic Survival Thriller

Jacqueline Druga

Copyright © 2022 Jacqueline Druga

All rights reserved

The characters and events portrayed in this book are fictitious. Any similarity to real persons, living or dead, is coincidental and not intended by the author.

No part of this book may be reproduced, or stored in a retrieval system, or transmitted in any form or by any means, electronic, mechanical, photocopying, recording, or otherwise, without express written permission of the publisher.

Special thanks to my team: Connie, Paula G, David D and Kira R.

For my ever supportive Pats!

ONE – DARK

June 17

I just wanted to go home.

I wanted my mother.

No matter how hard I tried, no matter what I did, I wasn't making progress.

For all I knew, we moved in circles.

There was no sun. None. At times, it was so dark, not even a flashlight made a difference.

Specks of hope came when, for a moment, the clouds parted, and I could see.

My hands hurt. My skin was so dry I could barely move my fingers. I was fearful of them bleeding with each clench of my fist, despite wearing gloves.

I wasn't freezing, not yet. It was coming. It seemed each hour the temperature dropped.

It was still the beginning of it all. I didn't want to think about what would happen in a week, a month, or even years.

If, of course, I lived that long.

Dying was an option. Not one I wanted to take, but one out of my control.

I didn't want to die. I really didn't. I just wanted to go home.

My entire life, I thought I was mature. Maybe I didn't act it, but I felt older than my teenage years.

Now, I don't. I'm scared.

As scared as any child in a dark bedroom, sitting on the bed, staring at the closet door screaming, "Mommy! Help!"

Crying out in some unfounded fear. Their chest holding back

a breath and being stuffed with a terror that was all too real to them.

Suddenly, I was that child. The terror was here. I could barely breathe.

My fear was not unfounded.

The world had become my monster in the closet.

TWO – THE MOVE

June 6 – Chadron, NE
TEN DAYS EARLIER

"The world will end in six days."

That was what the sign read. Big, blue letters; printed neatly, too. It was hard to miss, even though it was sandwiched between the words "milk" and "green onions" on the refrigerator white board.

My mother ignored it when she first saw it. It took me standing in front of that old fridge and pointing.

Then she said, "Marty, I think you're being a little melodramatic. Since you're standing there, grab me the milk, please. George wants dumplings."

Making me feel like my fears and concerns weren't valid.

She had proceeded to uproot and toss about my entire life, and she didn't bat an eye. Her attitude was military kids did it all the time.

We weren't military kids.

Not even close.

I liked living in Los Angeles. And even though we had only been in our new home two weeks, I hated it and wanted to go back.

My brother and I didn't have a choice in the matter. My little sister, Ruby, she was only three, and it didn't affect her. She didn't have friends, she didn't have a way of life, and she certainly wasn't in her sophomore year when Mom decided to say,

3

"Oh, by the way, we're moving to Nebraska."

What?

My sophomore year. Two years from graduating, and we were pulled from school.

It didn't bother my brother Ben. He really didn't care one way or another. He didn't have many friends. Any that he did have were a year ahead because he was held back in the second grade.

Ben was different.

Me, I was as normal as any fifteen-year-old girl could be.

I didn't understand why we had to move. Just because my stepfather had to quit his job and take over his father's farm.

Not that his dad had died. Pops was alive and physically fine. He just started to slip mentally, and it was time for George to take over.

I liked George for the longest time. I guess I still liked him. But I'm not happy with him because he was the reason we had to move.

When he met my mom, I was seven. My dad had died two years earlier. It was an accidental overdose of over-the-counter cold medicine and him drinking alcohol. At least that was what I was told. My father wrote for some television show. His residual royalties helped pay the bills.

It wasn't until George came around that I saw my mother smile again.

I mean, I actually never noticed she stopped smiling until she started again.

She said he saved our lives. But I know it was her life he saved. Even young, I was grateful. At the wedding, I called him my bonus father.

In hindsight, I didn't pay attention. It wasn't all of a sudden, we up and left. George was getting lots of calls about Pops and would have to go tend to business eventually.

I had even suggested they have a long-distance marriage for two years until Ben and I graduated.

It was quickly dismissed and did not go over well at all.

When my mother first said it was near Chadron City, I was

a little bit happier. At least it was a city. It wasn't until we arrived, and I realized there were more people in my former school district than the entire town of Chadron. And my mother was wrong, it wasn't even called a city.

But she said there was a Super Walmart, so it couldn't be that bad.

It was when the final decision to move came that it was rushed. Two weeks to wrap up my life, say goodbye, and trek halfway across the country like a "coming of age movie."

Ben said I was going through cultural shock.

No kidding.

I lived my entire life in an apartment. The closest thing we had to grass was the plants the property managers put by the pool.

From gray concrete to green.

Although Pops' house was pretty awesome, it wasn't modern. It was… country looking. Like a huge apartment, it was one floor with big rooms and more than one bathroom.

It had to be big because Pops was big. He was so tall, and he had a round middle. I once heard my mother say that Pops was one of the richest men in the county. You wouldn't know it to look at him. His gray hair was wiry and bushy, and he always wore overalls that were big even on him. When I was little, I thought he looked like a Teletubby.

Living with Pops was the positive in it all. He was always happy and laughed easily. Laughing to the point he made himself cough.

I didn't see the mental slippage everyone talked about. Maybe that just happened in the business aspect.

He was quick and didn't miss a thing. "Carly," he said to my mother. "How is she gonna get you milk if we need milk? The notes right there on the board above the news about the end of the world."

"There's enough in there to make dumplings," my mother replied.

Pops grumbled. His glasses perched on the end of his nose

as he looked at his tablet reader. "Who puts milk in dumplings? Must be a city thing."

I opened the fridge. "It's a delish-dot-com thing." I pulled out the nearly empty container of milk. "My mom had never made dumplings before."

"I'm sure they'll be delicious," Pops said. "And Marty, after you hand that milk to your mom, change that end of the world thing from six days to five. It went up yesterday, I don't want to think I have more days than I actually do." He started to laugh at his own humor. It started as a chuckle, rolled into a laugh, and ended with a cough.

He made me smile.

I kissed Pops on the cheek, handed the milk to my mom, then did as Pops suggested.

I changed it to, "The world ends in five days."

Not that the world was actually going to physically end, but for me … it sure felt like it.

THREE – NOT FOR ME

Time was running out. I had five days, and if I didn't think of something, I would be on a Chadron Church Youth Group bus headed to some summer camp, a hundred miles in west Wyoming.

I stared out the kitchen window plotting my move. I stared at George who was with Ben working on a fence. It was hard to see them as they were so far away. They could have been pretending to work.

"Leave him alone," my mother told me. "He's busy with that fence."

"Really, what teenager goes to summer camp?" I asked.

"A lot. A dozen from the church."

"What is up with that?" I asked. "We don't go to church. Why are we going with their youth group?"

"Because that's where the camp bus leaves from," my mother said. "You're lucky you have a seat. Honestly, Marty, stop. You'll regret giving us a hard time. It's an interactive camp."

"Mom, it's a camp. How can it not be interactive?"

Lifting his eyes from his book, Pops replied. "I'm sure you'll find a way."

"Marty," my mother said. "The camp has been around for decades. Your stepfather went to that camp."

"No offense, mom." I then looked at Pops. "No offense, but that doesn't make it cool. Did he go as a teenager?"

Pops replied. "Not at your age. I needed him here to work. He was not happy about that."

"I'll work," I said brightly. "I'll be happy to work on the farm."

"Ranch," Pops corrected. "And go. Hey, who knows? Maybe you'll be like Bobby Lee in 1972."

"Who's Bobby Lee? And why would I want to be like him?" I asked.

"He was the kid to spot and take a picture of Bigfoot."

I laughed. "Is that why it's named that?"

Pops nodded. "Yep. They changed the name the next year. Enrollment increased. They have daily scouting trips for the camp. But it's not called 'Camp Bigfoot' anymore. It's 'Camp Sasquatch.' Some group filed a lawsuit that it was politically incorrect or something to call it 'Bigfoot.'"

"Seriously? Calling something 'Bigfoot' is politically incorrect?" I asked in disbelief. "Mom, please don't make me go to this camp."

My mother sighed out. "You're going, and you'll like it. Trust me."

"I'm too old."

"You're not too old. It'll be a way for you and Ben to make some friends before the school year."

"At a summer camp?" I asked. "I'm sure there's another way to meet kids."

"You know …" Pops said. "I suggested yesterday for you and Ben to walk to the Super Walmart to meet other teenagers and you said—"

"Oh my God."

"That." Pops pointed at me. "You said that."

"That's because you suggested hanging out at the Walmart."

"Yeah," Pops replied. "Isn't that where teenagers hang out?"

"No. Walmart is not a teenage hang-out. Not even in Nebraska." I sighed. "There has to be another way."

"Your brother isn't complaining," my mother said.

"Ben only complains when his batteries die on his game controller." I looked out the window. "I'm not done, yet."

"Marty, leave your …."

I assumed my mother was telling me to leave my stepfather alone, but I was out the back door before she could finish.

George had to help me out. He was a nice guy.

Surely he could convince my mother that sending us away wasn't a good idea. He needed workers. Obviously, he was desperate because he had Ben helping fix a fence. Then again, my brother had this keen ability to look at something and fix it. Ben was bright like that. Everyone said it was because he was on the "spectrum" that he was able to do that. I claimed it was his genius talent.

My brother was a big kid. He looked even bigger compared to our class, because he was held back. He didn't talk much, was socially awkward, and if it wasn't for his size, he probably would have been picked on.

He had quirks that other kids laughed about behind his back.

When we were in grade school, I got into a lot of fights with kids laughing at him.

He was my brother. I fought with him. I picked on him, but nobody else was allowed.

I would defend him the rest of my life.

Now, it was payback. Ben had to get us out of going to the camp.

I made my way directly to them. I started to wonder how far away they actually were.

From the kitchen it was an optical illusion. Any farther, I'd need an Uber.

Maybe it was my imagination.

I certainly was out of breath.

"Marty," George laughed my name, and looked up when I approached. He lifted the rim to his old ball cap. "Did you walk all the way out here?"

"I did. I'm on a mission."

"Yeah, your mom sent me a text," he said. "It's about camp."

I grunted. "Really." I shook my head. "She cut me off before I could talk to you?"

"Marty …"

"Look, you have Ben working." I indicated to my brother. "I'll work the farm."

"Ranch," he corrected.

"Same difference."

George laughed. "No, it isn't. Farmers grow things. We raise things. 'Bushels and bales versus heads and tails'?"

"I have no idea what that means."

"It's means we don't grow food. We raise livestock," George said. "In particular… cattle."

"What if I work with those things." I pointed.

George looked over his shoulder. "You mean the horses?"

"Yeah."

"Marty, have you ever been close to a horse? I know you haven't since you got here. Why don't you walk over and see them?"

I looked at the dozen horses kinda meandering. "Nah, I'll pass." I turned to my brother. "Ben."

He didn't reply, he focused on the hinge.

"Ben." I paused, then said his name louder. "Ben!"

"What?" he looked up.

"You know you'll be going a week without video games."

"You're funny," Ben replied. "You didn't look at the brochure. They have video tournaments. A giant video wall."

George chuckled. "It's not 1985, the year they banned Atari. They have all kinds of fun stuff."

I looked back at Ben. "I suppose you read about looking for bigfoot, too?"

"Sasquatch," Ben corrected. "Bigfoot is politically incorrect."

"Why aren't you upset about this?" I asked.

"It's one week," Ben said. "It's better than hanging out at the Walmart."

"No one hangs out at the Walmart," I said.

"Is that so?" asked George. "I thought all the kids hung out there."

"No!"

"Look, I'll make you a deal," said George. "That camp is fun. Especially if you have the right attitude. I went."

"Not when you were our age."

"And I was mad about that," George replied. "Trust me; I liked it. I wanted to go. So my deal is this." He leaned on the fence. "Two days. You go out there. Two days, two sleeps."

"Sleeps?" I laughed. "What am I? Three."

"Two sleeps," George continued. "And if you aren't having fun, and you want to leave, I will come and get you."

Ben spoke up. "I'm telling mom."

"Shut up," I snapped then smiled at George. "Deal. Thank you."

"However..." George continued. "You have to stop whining and complaining about it and stop confusing my dad with this 'world is gonna end' stuff written on the shopping list."

"Pops isn't confused by that."

"Oh, yeah?" George raised an eyebrow. "Why did he take a bunch of stuff to the storm cellar this morning?"

"Okay, I'll erase it and tell..." I stopped talking when several of the horses did this weird cry out. I knew it was called a 'neigh,' but it sounded freaky. And it was as if something had scared them.

Suddenly, all of the horses, at the same time, appeared as if they were trying to run backwards, hitting into each other. They did that for a second or two, still making that loud noise before they quieted down and ran top speed around the perimeter of the fence.

"Okay," I said. "Scratch what I said before. I don't want to work with them."

George stared back in the fenced in area. "Strange."

"That's not normal?" I asked.

He shook his head.

"Maybe there's an earthquake coming," Ben suggested. "I heard animals act weird."

"They do. Maybe it is an earthquake." George shrugged and replied nonchalantly.

"In Nebraska?" I asked.

"Could happen," George said.

"Yep. And if it does, I'll go straight down and hang with all the kids that supposedly hang at Walmart," I said sarcastically, then literally took two steps away from that fence when I felt the familiar rumble of the ground beneath my feet.

The buzz. The vibration.

It wasn't long. Ten seconds. But it certainly was a tremor, and it caused the horses to react again.

"Whoa." George looked up with a smile. "How about that? I'll take you to Walmart when we're done."

George and my brother both laughed.

I didn't. But I couldn't get mad. George made that deal, and he was a man of his word. I was still going to that summer camp, but at least it was only for two days.

FOUR – ERASER

June 10

"So, you understand," I said. "It's all on you."

My baby sister sat on my bed, her back against the pillow, while I lay on my stomach talking to her. She had asked if she could sleep in my room; and since I was leaving the next morning, I didn't mind.

I adored Ruby.

Yeah, at first it creeped me out that my mom was having a baby, considering I knew where babies came from. And I thought for sure I would have to be the babysitter, but it wasn't the case.

I was so happy. She didn't look like me or Ben. More like George with the blonde hair and big green eyes.

Her bangs needed cut and they went into her eyes. She'd lift her pudgy little hand to pull them back.

"So tomorrow I'm leaving," I told her.

Ruby shook her head. "No, Muddy, no leave."

I loved when she called me "Muddy." Maybe because I knew one day she would say my name correctly and the cuteness would be gone.

"Sissy, I won't be away long," I said. "Two sleeps."

"Two?"

"Two."

"Okay."

"You have to remember. You can't like it here. You have to tell mom you don't like it here."

"I like it here," she said. "I like the grass."

"Yeah, I guess that's pretty cool."

"You gonna get your jammies on?" Ruby asked. "Can we watch a movie?"

"Yes and yes." I rolled over just when there was a knock on the archway of my open door.

Pops stood there. He held a plate, and his tablet was tucked under his arm.

"Hey, Pops." My eyes shifted to the plate. "Is that chocolate cake?"

"It is. We hit the Super Walmart tonight. I tried to make you some friends while we were there. Didn't turn out well. I got arrested."

I laughed. "You're funny."

"Thanks. Anyhow… who erased the warning?"

"The warning?"

"You know, the end-of-the-world warning. It was on the fridge."

"Oh, yeah. George said I had to erase it."

"He did, huh?" Pops asked. "Well, I fixed it. You had the world ending tomorrow the eleventh. The guy on my forum red-edit group gave a more compelling reason for it to end on the fifteenth."

"Red-edit? You mean Reddit."

"Yes, that's it."

"Some guy on Reddit said the world is ending on the fifteenth?"

"Not just any guy. Reed Collins. Big scientist."

"Okay, that makes it better. Thanks."

"You're welcome. Good night. And don't worry. When you get back, if you can't find us, we'll be in the storm cellar. I'll have it all stocked up."

"Thank you."

After he had walked away, Ruby glanced up to me with sad eyes and spoke in an innocent almost whining voice. "Muddy, I don't want the world to end."

"No worries, Sissy. It's not. Pops is playing around." I kissed her forehead. "Hey, want some cake?"

She nodded quickly.

"Stay here. I'll be right back." I rolled off the bed and stood. Looking back at Ruby, I grabbed my stuffed backpack for camp to put in the living room, then walked out. Passing Ben's room, I thought about asking if he wanted cake, but he was sound asleep.

I walked down the hall and through the living room. I set my bag next to Ben's by the front door. Seeing my mom and George there made me laugh. They each sat in a chair, a table lamp between them. It reminded me of the old sitcoms and the way married people sat after supper. But instead of newspapers, they both were diligently into their phones. Probably liking each other's posts on social media.

"Hey," I announced as I walked through. "I'm gonna grab me and Ruby some cake if that's okay?"

My mom looked over at me. "Sure. George picked it up at Walmart when he went to get Ben some socks for camp."

"Yeah, Pops told me you guys went. He joked he got arrested."

George glanced at me with a serious look.

"Wait? Did Pops get arrested?" I asked.

"Close," George answered. "He decided to make you some friends and approached a girl about your age. She took it the wrong way, as you can imagine. She started screaming stranger danger. Security came. But thankfully, the Sheriff was able to set things straight with her mom."

"Oh my God, poor Pops. Was he super upset?"

George shook his head. "Mad."

"I'm sorry."

"It's not your fault," George said. "We all need to watch what we say. He's taking things very literal now."

"I get it. I'll be careful. Right now…" I pointed back. "I'm getting cake."

Only the light above the sink was on when I walked in, and I turned on the overhead light. After grabbing a plate and forks,

I looked for the cake. I didn't see it on the table or the counter. Figuring someone put it away, I walked to the fridge and reached for the door.

I paused before opening it when I saw the white board.

In Pops' handwriting was written, "The world will end on June 15th."

At that moment, instead of laughing, I felt bad for Pops. I didn't think my little rant on the grocery list would affect him so much.

I thought about erasing it but changed my mind. I didn't need to confuse him more.

I grabbed cake for me and Ruby and went back to my room to try to enjoy something before I left for that stupid camp.

FIVE – ROLLING ALONG

June 11

I couldn't sleep. I tossed and turned. Even Ruby's foot in my face didn't disturb me as much as my dream. A bus full of overly happy, bible-study teenagers on a short bus to camp. All loud; singing ninety-nine bottles of root beer on the wall, instead of beer because that would just be wrong. Even the Ben in my dream was laughing, smiling, and singing. That was how I knew it was a dream because that just wasn't Ben.

After very little sleep, it was time to go. I knew I was tired because even my bookbag felt heavier than I remembered.

My mother was cheerful, hugging us both, telling us to have fun.

Of course, she was happy; she was getting rid of us.

I was dreading what was ahead. Dreading meeting the kids of Chadron who all belonged to some youth-group cult together, and their highlight of the year was going to the bigfoot camp.

They probably all wore matching shirts and hats and would squeal in delight when they saw each other.

Dread.

Just kill me, kill me now, I thought when we pulled from the driveway.

George drove us.

He said, "I'll let you in on a little secret. The bus doesn't leave for ninety minutes."

Did he actually think we would be happy to hear we woke up earlier than we needed to?

Then he told us he wanted to take us to breakfast at Bob Evans, just like Pops used to do with him when he'd leave for camp.

I couldn't be mad. A hot breakfast sounded good and was better than the Pop Tart my mother handed me when I walked out the door. I slipped the strawberry pastry in the front pocket of my bag, in case the food at camp sucked.

"It won't be that bad," George told us, after breakfast and on our way to the bus. "Really, it won't be. A little confusing; but if there's problems you can call. It's only a hundred and two miles."

"You always liked going?" I asked.

"Yes. It was fun," George replied. "It's a great learning experience and the theme is finding sasquatch. I think you'll be surprised."

"I doubt it," I said.

"What about you, Ben?" George asked. "You excited?"

Ben shrugged.

"It's been a minute," George said. "But when you get there, they'll have someone waiting. You'll give them your name, find your cabin, and then everyone meets up."

"How far will I be from Ben?" I asked. "They don't do some super separation thing, do they? I really don't want to be far from him."

"Oh, I don't know," George replied. "When I went there, they did. But things change. I don't know."

Finally, it was time. I really didn't know the town of Chadron, and I assumed that gray building was the church. When we pulled in the back lot, the short white bus was parked there.

There were a lot of cars; parents with kids.

I really didn't look at the kids too much, figuring I'd see them enough when they annoyed me on the bus.

George parked and helped us out. He gave us both hugs.

"Make sure your phones are always charged, and call us," he instructed.

He stood back, not wanting to embarrass us by hovering.

Ben and I shouldered our bags.

"Mine really feels heavy," I said to Ben about my bag. "Does yours?"

He shrugged.

Of course, he did. He always said very little.

"Hey," I whispered as we walked. "Don't get too far from me. Okay?"

"Where am I gonna go, Marty? I'm right here."

He was.

I looked at the mini school bus. It could have been gray instead of white, because all I saw was a prison bus. It would take us away, lock us up from civilization, and make us do things I would cringe about the rest of my life.

I wondered what was going through Ben's mind as we walked to that bus. It didn't seem to faze him at all.

He behaved like it was an everyday event for him, just like school back in LA. His backpack was not one-shoulder like I carried mine, Ben had his on his back. The only thing that told me Ben was nervous was his blinking.

My brother blinked a lot when he was uncomfortable.

Approaching that bus, Ben blinked.

The bus driver wore a "Camp Sasquatch" tee shirt. Red, with a silkscreen image of Bigfoot that looked like an old school Stalin shirt.

He held a clipboard. "Bags there, thanks. Just leave them on the ground," he said and pointed. The hatch to the undercarriage storage area was open. We set them down. I didn't put my name on my bag. I hoped my mother did.

We approached the camp clipboard man.

"Ben and Marty Lowe," I said.

"Oh, hey; yeah, the new kids. Welcome."

I grumbled a little under my breath, then looked over my shoulder at George as I stepped on the bus.

George leaned against the truck, arms folded and watching us.

I lifted two fingers to him to signify two days as I led the way, first one on, and decided where we'd sit.

I didn't want to sit up front and feared harassment by the wannabe cool kids if we sat in the back. So I picked the fourth row, which was right in the middle.

"You want the window or aisle?" I asked Ben.

"I don't care."

That being said, I slipped in first and took the window seat. I would pretend to look outside; but really I was watching the other kids get on so I could judge them.

They probably would judge me and Ben.

My brother played on his phone. He didn't care.

They boarded one by one. But instead of bracing to be annoyed, I was kind of surprised.

There was no loud, overzealous chatter. A few of the boys wore headphones or ear buds, plopping into a seat, looking as tired as I felt.

The one boy across from us never looked away from his phone when he sat down. He just did what I had seen other kids do a hundred times on the school buses back in LA: Sat with his knees against the seat before him as he slouched, burying his head in his phone.

Two girls around my age walked down the aisle. They stayed close, probably friends. They spoke in whispering voices, a giggle here and there. Not at anyone on the bus, but something said between them.

As they passed me, the one looked and gave a genuine closed mouth smile. One of acknowledgement or a hello.

Only a dozen kids entered the bus. Only two weren't teenagers.

My worries were unfounded, and I judged too harshly. So far, there was nothing different about the kids that got on the bus.

Some, like me, looked like they didn't even want to go.

They didn't dress weird or act weird.

The bus driver got on the bus, did another head count, then asked if we were ready.

A couple kids replied loudly, but most were mumbles.

After his instruction to "buckle up", he took the driver's seat and closed the door.

I looked out the window for real and saw George. He stood by the truck. He hadn't left and probably wouldn't until we rolled away.

There was a comfort about seeing him there. I knew he cared.

Not sure if he could see me, I lifted my hand and placed it against the window.

My way to wave once more.

As the bus started moving, George waved.

He didn't move even as we did.

The small bus was quiet. The kids weren't annoying, at least not yet.

Maybe George was right. Maybe it wouldn't be so bad after all.

SIX – CAMP SASQUATCH

Niobrara County, Wyoming

A hundred miles later, we arrived. We stopped for a bathroom break just after the "Welcome to Wyoming" sign. I heard the camp was two miles before a place called Lusk. I had never heard of it.

I had a hard time believing there was a campsite anywhere. Most of the trip I looked at dirt outside with very little green.

Maybe there wasn't grass; I just thought Bigfoot needed trees and grass.

Sure enough, when the bus driver announced we were there, we turned on a road that was treelined and forest-like.

It was what I thought a campsite should look like. Another bus passed us going the opposite way; just as we pulled in.

It was then everyone on the bus started to perk up. I looked out the window, trying to see.

"Everyone out," the driver said as he stood before us. "We're here. You can grab your bags after I unload them. Mister Sam is waiting for you."

Ben waited for all the other kids to pass. I was happy about that. It gave me a chance to see how things went.

When we stepped off, the bus driver was unloading our bags.

"You okay?" I asked my brother.

"Yeah. I'm fine. You?"

"Wow. You asked how I was."

"Stop."

"Okay, I'm good."

Then we met Mister Sam.

He stood before us; a typical camp guy with a clipboard in his hand, but he was far from typical. In every summer camp movie I had seen, the big-wig camp guy was some nerdy and skinny man with tan shorts, white tube socks, and possibly a fanny pack.

Not Mister Sam.

He looked like he should have been on television, playing a rock star. He wore his red Camp Sasquatch tee shirt, a pair of jeans, and he had really cool, slightly longer dark hair that came to just above his shoulders.

Sam wasn't a kid either, he was probably close to George's age.

"Hey, everyone. Welcome to Camp Sasquatch. I'm Mister Sam," he said. "You can call me Sam, if you want. I know some of you are excited, and some are not. Some are new… some are not. Welcome. You're gonna have a great time. We're still waiting on two more buses. But feel free to go unpack. For you new people, behind me…" he pointed backwards. There were two buildings a hundred feet away. One large and one smaller. "Those are the only WIFI spots in the entire camp. Only place you will get a signal. The rec-slash-dining room and the office."

I pulled out my phone and looked at it.

"Have to get closer," Sam said. "Now, we don't want you on your phones or tablets, so WIFI is only on at meals and an hour in the evening."

Everyone groaned.

"Come on, you won't even miss the world," he continued. "The cabins, as some of you know, are beyond the buildings and across the campfire area. Our cabins are there as well. Sasquatchas, you ladies are in cabin six. Sasquatchos, you are in Cabin two. Tish will be your counselor. I'll be with the guys. Go unpack. Feel free after unpacking to hit the rec room and check in at home."

I looked at Ben. "Sasquatchos and Sasquatchas. He knows sasquatch is not Spanish, right?"

"Does it matter?" Ben asked. "He's trying to be funny."

"Hmm."

As I started to walk, a girl from the bus caught up to us and as she walked by, stated, "Tish is the best one. We're so lucky."

Ben turned his head to me. "Who was that?"

I shrugged.

The girl spun around. "I'm Carla," she shouted, then turned back around, racing toward the cabin.

"She heard you," I told him.

We made it through the buildings, following the other kids.

The cabin area was nice. They all had big, wide porches on each one.

I didn't know if that was normal or not because it was the first time in my life I ever saw a cabin outside pictures or movies.

"See you at the rec building?" I asked Ben as we parted.

"I'll meet you there."

I thanked him, not sure why, and then I found my cabin.

It was bigger than I expected and nice inside.

Log cabin walls, a picnic-style table by the front window with a couch. And eight single, cot-style beds, lined the walls. Four on each side. Each had a small two drawer dresser at the foot of the bed.

"Bathroom and showers are in the back." Carla said, pointing to a door at the end of the room. "Showers were put in last year. We used to have to go near the rec hall to get a shower. Take any cot. No one cares."

"Thanks." I put my bag on the bed.

"Here. You might need this to get around." Carla handed me what looked like a brochure. "There's a map of the camp inside. This is my fifth year."

"Fifth? You must like it," I said.

"I love it."

I finally looked at her, really looked at her. She was the one that smiled at me on the bus. She had her dark blonde hair pulled back in a ponytail. She was my height and size.

"Your name?" she asked.

"Oh, sorry. Marty."

"Oh, I like that. You got on at the church. I never saw you in school."

"We just moved here."

She winced. "Sorry about that."

I chuckled a little and unzipped my bag. As soon as I did, I knew why it felt heavier. Crammed in there was a clear plastic bag. In it, from what I could see, were two bottles of water, and it looked like one of those pouches of food. There was more.

"You brought a go bag?"

"A what?"

"Go bag, bug-out bag. Supplies you need in case you have to get out fast and survive on the run."

I closed my eyes. "No, I didn't put this in here. My grandfather did."

"Does he think a plague is hitting."

"What?" I asked, confused.

She tapped the bag. "There's masks in there."

I shook my head. "I don't know."

"Is he one of those crazy survival people?"

"No. He has dementia."

"I'm sorry."

"It's okay, I'm gonna…" I lifted my phone. "Go check in. I'll be right back."

"Sure."

Before I walked out, I shoved the go bag back in the bookbag and zipped it up.

<><><><>

George answered the phone with a bright and happy, "Hey! You made it!"

"We did."

"We were watching you on the tracker. You went out of range

right before Lusk."

"That's because there's only a signal and WIFI in the dining hall or whatever," I said.

"Where's Ben?" George asked.

"Unpacking. George... hey, I really feel bad. I didn't mean to make things worse."

"What do you mean?"

"Pops," I said sadly. "I wrote that note and he is really taking this serious now. He put a bug-out bag in my book bag."

"Yeah, he um, told me about that. He said he even spent all night marking a safe route home on the map."

"I didn't mean to..."

"Stop," George said. "I don't want you to worry. This might not be a bad thing. He's not just sitting there staring out the window or reading the same article over and over. He's staying busy. He's learning stuff and talking to people on the Red-Edit group."

"Reddit."

"Yes. So, you don't worry. If he starts planning to cause the apocalypse, then we will do something. Right now, he's, like I said, staying busy."

"Are you sure?"

"Positive. You focus on making friends and having fun."

"Is mom there?"

"She's getting her hair done. Call later?"

"I will."

"Hey, I love you guys," George said. "Try to make it work."

"I will, and I love you, too."

After the call, I didn't feel better. I still felt bad. I didn't get the dementia thing. How something so simple like a joking note on the fridge could send someone into such a state that they suddenly were completely delusional.

I didn't know how long I'd end up staying at camp, but I knew once I got home, I was going to work with Pops. I caused his instant apocalypse obsession; I could get him out of it.

SEVEN – SHAKING

June 15 - Lusk, WY

My brother laughed.

Second dinner at camp, soggy tacos as the meal, and I heard my brother laugh.

It wasn't a fake laugh; it was genuine and loud. I was seated at the girls table, and I looked across the dining room. Ben was with three boys, all of them laughing and making jokes.

In the fifteen years I had known my brother, I had only heard him laugh out loud twice.

Not often and not recently.

Yet, there he was, and it was the first time he just was a normal teenage boy. His nose wasn't buried in his phone. His body language didn't scream antisocial. Maybe there was something about the kids in LA that never really brought Ben out of it. Perhaps it was the simplicity of the summer camp.

Whatever it was, I couldn't leave.

If I left, Ben would leave; and I didn't want to take my brother away from the one situation he felt at ease.

So, we stayed.

I snapped a picture of my smiling brother and sent it to my mother with a message saying Ben was having a great time and I wasn't leaving.

It really wasn't a bad time. I loved going to the lake, even though I refused to really get in because I was scared to death of flesh-eating bacteria. I enjoyed the hunt for Sasquatch and hearing the story about Bobby Lee as we took to the trails.

I wanted to find Bigfoot. I did, and I really thought we would.

Summer camp wasn't lame arts and crafts and badly acted plays. It wasn't teenage angst and hormones, like you see in the movies.

It was a genuinely fun time. I wouldn't go as far as to say I made a lot of friends. I was friendly, and I liked Carla. Even though she talked a lot and snored pretty loudly for a girl her size.

They kept us busy, and Carla and I signed up for the field trip into Lusk.

Ben didn't. He stayed back to play arrows or whatever it was called.

I was more curious about taking a field trip at Summer Camp. Wasn't camp itself a field trip?

The town of Lusk was eight miles away, and a portion of it was dedicated to the history of the western expansion.

There was a wagon wheel museum, a mock trade store, a settlers' exhibition, and a corner restaurant with a flashing neon sign illuminated in the day which said "Donner Party Diner".

I didn't understand what it meant until Tish told us about the Donner Party. A part of me wanted to eat there and a part of me didn't.

We took the mini-bus for the small group of us that wanted to go. Then again, that was the only bus there. The camp owned that one, the others were rented out.

When we walked into the wagon wheel museum, the souvenir ticket stub made me pause when I saw the date.

June fifteenth.

I immediately pulled out my phone and set a text to my mother, "Tell Pops I said hello."

Instead of a simply "OK" or a reply stating she'd tell him, she asked why I was able to text.

"Just tell him I said hi and am thinking about him," I replied. "I'm on a field trip."

Then I put my phone back in my pocket.

"Everything okay?" Carla asked.

"Yeah. Just texting my mom. You know, since we have a signal."

"That's cool you randomly text your mom," Carla said. "My mom would freak. We fight all the time. She's nice. I mean, but she works at the Walmart, and when she works nights, I can't hang out there without her…"

"Whoa. Whoa. Wait." I held up my hand. "Hang out where?"

"The Walmart."

"Why do you hang out at the Walmart?"

"Everyone does. Friday nights or summer. It's something to do. Where do kids hang out in LA?"

"Not the Walmart," I said.

"Oh, it's the only place. Plus, you can buy cheap food," Carla said. "Once in a while you get the creepers. Like last week, some old guy tried to kidnap me."

"Oh my God!"

"Yeah, he pretended he needed me to find his granddaughter. I just yelled out…"

"Stranger Danger?"

Carla stopped walking. "Did I tell you this story before?"

"No, I was just… you know, that's the thing we are taught to do."

"Right." She nodded, then paused at a covered wagon.

It was big. The size surprised me.

"It looks real," I said.

"It is real," Carla replied. "Last year's guide said it's in perfect working condition. Then again, there's no electronics. Look at these wheels." She touched it. "Like they took people across the country. Before roads. People made it thousands of miles in just this thing. Through snow and rain." Carla sighed out.

"You really like this?"

"I do. I come to the tour every year. Sometimes I hope for something new to be here."

"Carla," I laughed. "This stuff is from hundreds of years ago. I don't think they're getting anything new."

"You never know. They might dig something up."

Carla smiled, but than her smile froze and suddenly dropped.

It started out with a rumble, like a tractor trailer rolling down the road, but it increased in intensity as the floor beneath our feet vibrated.

The lights flickered, and just before everything shook, the windows rattled. The ear-shattering loudness of the breaking glass and the howling roar that mimicked beating drums was frightening.

"What's happening?" Carla screamed.

I grabbed her arm as I answered., "Earthquake. We need to get out."

I raced with my friend toward the door as the floor moved in waves. It was hard to keep my footing. I swayed left to right, and it caused me to run diagonally.

I had been in an earthquake before. Nothing major though, but it didn't feel like the one I had experienced. This quake felt different.

People screamed loudly and ran just as we did.

Once outside, we headed toward the street. Carla was fine until a car lost control in front of us, slamming into a parked car.

That's when Carla lost it.

I needed to get us away from windows. Away from falling debris.

Standing in the road, I watched traffic lights swing violently, telephone poles sway, and windows shatter.

Then it stopped.

The shaking, the noise… it all just stopped.

It halted for a moment before, like an added little burp, there was one more jolt.

Then it was over.

Car alarms sounded off from all over, and the now dark neon sign of the Donner Party Diner told me the power had gone down.

"Where are my campers?" Tish asked. "Sasquatch campers!" she shouted. "I need my eleven! Check in!"

Carla and I raced over to the bus.

"Here," I said. "We're here."

Tish put her hand on her chest. "Oh my God. Are you alright?"

I nodded.

Not long after we showed up, others did, too.

Tish counted heads, making sure everyone was there.

"What happened?" someone asked.

"I think it was an earthquake," Tish replied, then looked at me. "You're from California. Do you know if it was?"

"That was definitely an earthquake," I answered.

Suddenly everyone was gathering around me, asking me questions, all at the same time. It was too much; I couldn't understand them. The merged voices created this weird hum.

"Everyone!" Tish called out, bringing a silence to those around me. "Let's just get back on the bus. We'll head back." She had her phone, dialed it, and put it to her ear. Just as fast, she pulled it away and lowered it to look. Her fingers swiped and her expression suddenly changed.

She looked worried, almost scared.

"What is it?" I asked her.

Tish shook her head. "Nothing. Let's just head back. Get on the bus."

Carla and I were near the end of the line to board. I pulled out my phone. I wanted to text Ben or call my mom.

Glancing at the right-hand corner, I saw I had a signal. I hit my mom's name and hit "call". Even as I listened, I heard nothing.

Looking at my phone, it said "call failed".

I tried again... nothing.

Three times, I made an attempt.

The call would not go through.

EIGHT – HAPPENING

Camp Sasquatch, WY

Tish drove like a madman, way faster back to camp than she did on the way to Lusk. I understood her panic over the earthquake. They were scary and she probably never had experienced one before. She needed to know running didn't make a difference. In fact, it was dangerous because the roads could have buckled or cracked. At the rate of speed she drove, she would have hit the damaged pavement before she registered seeing it.

Luckily, she didn't, and we made it back to the campsite.

It seemed like every counselor was waiting for us. The six of them, plus Sam, stood where the bus would park.

The only kid I saw was my brother.

That made me worry.

Had something happened with my brother that they had to pull him away from the others?

Immediately, my mind went back to the fourth grade, when Ben was picked on so bad. It even got physical.

It stayed that way until he got bigger than everyone.

As soon as we stepped from the bus, Sam called out. "Can you guys all go back to your cabins, please? Thank you. Pretend it's a rain day."

I hated when this happened. Adults being secretive. We weren't little kids. And what the heck was a rain day?

"What's a rain day!" I yelled out.

"When it rains," Sam replied.

"No kidding!"

Carla walked over to me. "It means you stay inside and play games. Usually, we're allowed in the rec room." She shrugged.

I watched as she walked away, then saw the counselors huddled together as they kept looking at us and moved toward the office.

Ben walked over to me. "Are you okay?"

I nodded. "You?"

"Yeah, we heard about the quake."

"It was crazy. I didn't think they had earthquakes here. Did you feel anything up here?"

"Oh, yeah; we felt it. Jerry nearly hit Sam with an arrow, because he was shooting when it started."

I couldn't help it; that made me laugh.

One of the male counselors hollered out, "To the cabins, please." But I didn't know which one.

Ben grabbed my arm, leading me toward the cabin area. "Something is going on, Mart."

"No kidding," I replied. "We had an earthquake."

"No… something," he spoke in a low voice. "They just…"

"What?"

He stopped talking. Was something wrong? Was someone around?

"Ben?"

"We have to go in our cabins now. I'll tell you later when we can come out."

That was so typically Ben. He took everything literally. When they said go to the cabin, like a well programmed soldier, he was planning on doing just that.

"No! You can't just leave it at that!" I snapped, then grabbed his arm and pulled him.

"Where are we going?"

"We'll talk in my cabin."

"Boys aren't allowed in the girl cabins."

"Who cares? It doesn't count. You're my brother."

I dragged him up the two steps and inside. "Here. Sit down." I pointed to the table. It was out of earshot and near the window.

"We'll pretend we're playing a game; in case a counselor comes by. They can see us." I reached for the chess board off the shelf and put it on the table.

Ben sat and immediately started setting up the board. "What if they yell?"

"They won't yell."

"What if they kick us out?"

"They won't. I'll just tell them I had to be with you because of your condition."

"What condition?" Ben asked.

"You know. Your spectrum thing."

"Technically, it's not a condition."

"Technically, it is," I retorted.

"Not really."

"Whatever."

"Hey!" Macy yelled out. "He's not supposed to be in here."

"Shut up! It doesn't count. He's my brother."

"You don't have to be rude."

"Apologize," Ben whispered.

"Sorry!" I hollered and sat across from him. "Go on." I grabbed a piece and moved it.

"Anyhow… wait," Ben said. "You can't move a pawn diagonally."

"What difference does it make?"

"It's a pawn, they don't move diagonally. They moved forward. Two spaces on the first move…"

"It doesn't matter, Ben."

"Yeah, it does. That's not how you play chess," he said.

"I have no idea how to play chess."

"Then why did you pull it out?"

"So it looks like we're playing a game," I told him.

"Then you should have picked a game you know how to play."

"Why does it matter if we're only pretending?"

"Because chess is a game of integrity."

"Oh my God."

Ben shook his head. "I can't believe George didn't teach you. Wait, I can see why…"

"Ben!" I slammed my hand on the table.

Ben jolted then shook his head again. "Now, see? You're just knocking things over."

"Ben, what happened?" I asked.

"If you're gonna argue," Macy said. "I'm telling."

"Then tell. God!" I stared at my brother.

Ben moved a piece and leaned in, dropping his voice. "So, it started before the quake. It was weird. Make a move."

It took a second to register what he meant, so I moved what I now knew was a pawn.

"We were at archery, and that old pager thing that Sam wears, it starts buzzing, right?"

"That never buzzes unless Miss Ruth is calling him from the office."

"Exactly. So, he starts to head back, and there's Miss Ruth, running toward her car. He calls her, 'Miss Ruth, Miss Ruth, what's going on? What's wrong?'"

"What did she say?"

"She yells out as she is running that she left a note on the desk and has to get to her family."

"Did she have an emergency?" I asked. "Someone died?"

"That's what I thought. You know, something happened at home. Sam said hold off. No one was to shoot until he came back. We were right by the office, and Sam goes in. When he comes out…" Ben paused to move a piece. "He was texting someone and looked like he saw a ghost. He looked scared."

"Maybe he knew the person that died."

Ben shrugged. "I don't know. He started calling us in, walking like a zombie. And then the earthquake hit. After it was over, he was telling us, 'Everyone to your cabins'. I wasn't going. Especially when I saw all of them grouped together."

"You mean the counselors?"

Ben nodded. "They knew something bad."

"What could it be? You know, Tish had that same look on her

face when she looked at her phone after the earthquake."

"Bet it was Sam's text," Ben said. "There was no signal after that."

"It's so weird," I said.

When I said that, it was like Carla thought I was talking to her because she made this odd comment, as if she had been eavesdropping. But that wasn't the case.

"Yeah, it is weird," she said. "Look, it's snowing."

With a snap, I turned back to look at her. She was behind me staring out the other window.

"Is it cold enough to snow?" Carla asked.

Turning my head, I looked out the window.

Small white flakes floated down. It wasn't a lot, nor did they move fast. Sporadic flakes here and there, floating down.

After looking at Ben, he and I both stood up, left the table, and walked out.

I stayed focus on the courtyard area between the cabins, looking at the flakes. I stepped off the porch and held out my hand, hoping to catch one.

There weren't that many, and I had to maneuver my right hand so one would fall into my palm.

It looked gray instead of white and it certainly didn't melt the second it hit my hand.

I touched it, rubbing it with my left-hand index finger.

It wasn't soft, it wasn't cold. It was coarse.

It wasn't snow that fell… it was ash.

NINE – EVESDROPPING MADE EASY

I had never seen snow in my life. Just like I had never seen a skunk. And though I had never seen either of them, it didn't mean I didn't know the difference between when it was snow and when it was a skunk.

I have seen ash.

Coming off a fire in the pit after burning, during the wildfires in California.

I knew ash. But this, what remained in my palm, was different.

It didn't feel soft and fluffy.

"Marty?" Ben called my name.

"Where is it coming from?" I asked softly.

"Marty."

I looked up. "Where's it coming from, Ben? Do you think maybe something caught fire in town?"

Ben shook his head. "Remember two weeks ago when we moved to Pops? Remember he lit a bonfire in the backyard and burned the boxes from our move?"

I nodded.

"When did the ash rise?"

"I don't know."

"When the box turned to ash, and the wind blew it at us. Like an ash on a cigarette. Ash doesn't appear until something has burned."

"What's burning?" I asked.

"I don't know."

I felt a sense of urgency. An urgency that cried to me that I needed to find out at that very second, and I didn't know why.

Stepping farther into the large area between the cabins, I looked at the campfire pit to see if the ash was coming from there. But I knew better. I know it wasn't blowing from somewhere on the campsite. It was falling slowly from the sky.

I peered up to the sky looking for smoke. But it was hard to see beyond the trees that rose higher than the cabins.

Lowering my head to look at Ben, I noticed the others coming from the cabin, reaching in awe for the ash and acting like it was the first snowfall of the season.

Maybe it was nothing. Maybe it was normal. Maybe some rancher a few miles out was actually burning something. It was odd timing. Really odd timing.

The earthquake, the counselors acting strange, now the falling ash.

"Ben, do you think we should tell Sam and the others about this?" I asked.

"They probably already know."

"Still… I mean, they told us to go to the cabins. There is definitely something they aren't telling us."

"It won't hurt," Ben replied. "Let's go."

Ben and I slipped away from the others, taking the path to the office cabin.

The counselors were all gathered in there, meeting about something.

Granted, it could have had nothing to do with the earthquake. Maybe there was a financial thing, or the food had rats.

Worse. What if one of the kids was missing?

I didn't bother to check. Then again, I wouldn't know who wasn't present.

There were a lot of reasons to worry the counselors that had nothing to do with the earthquake.

It could have been coincidental timing.

I could see the rear of the office cabin ahead of us, and just as we were about ten feet away, Ben stopped me. He placed his finger to his lips to make sure I was quiet.

I didn't understand why until I heard the muffled voices of the counselors.

Slowly, we crept closer, and the voices were clearer.

Their voices meshed together, talking over one another. Their tone seemed to be on the cusp of stress.

Ben mouthed the words, "Let's just listen."

And we did. I didn't get why Ben wanted to listen before we told them about the ash.

"It's insane," a woman said. "All this waiting."

"I don't have a signal yet," another said.

"Me either. I just checked the WIFI. Nothing."

"Can you please radio the Sheriff?" Tish asked. "Sam, please."

"I tried," Sam replied. "You heard him. He said he'd radio back."

"And that's all he said," Tish stated. "Radio him again. It's been twenty minutes. Get him to talk to you."

"Fine. Fine," Sam replied.

Was that what they were doing? Arguing back and forth. Needing a call from the sheriff.

There were a few seconds of silence until I heard Sam's voice. "Camp Sasquatch calling Niobrara County sheriff, come in."

There was a low key hissing sound.

"Camp Sasquatch calling Niobrara County sheriff, do you read?"

It was eerie.

No voices, just a long stream of white noise.

"This is Camp Sasquatch, calling Niobrara County Sheriff, are you there?"

Hiss.

Static.

"Hey, Sam," came another voice, this one sounded like it came through a speaker. "This is Sheriff Davidson, I hear you."

"Sheriff, thank you."

"We'll get back to you. I told you that last time," the sheriff said.

"I know you said that. I need answers."

"We don't have any to give."

"We're concerned, Sheriff. We have one small bus and sixty-four kids up here. We need to get them out," Sam said.

"I know you do. And we will. I told you that. I am working on it, but there is a shit load of problems in Lusk right now."

"I get it, I do," Sam replied. "My people are worried. Time is of the essence."

"Sam, you know as well as I do, time is on our side," the sheriff said. "You got the same alert I did. It's early. It could be days, it could be weeks; heck, it could be years. Rest assured; we'll get those kids out. Let me do my job down here so we can get to you up there."

"I understand. Thank you, sheriff."

"Over."

The voices of the counselors resumed, talking loudly over each other.

"Enough!" yelled Sam, "You heard him. We wait."

"It's crazy," Tish said.

"We have time." Sam replied. "We have time."

"Do we?" Tish asked. "Should we really assume we have time?"

"What do you want me to do, Tish?" Sam snapped. "Huh? There's nothing we can do. Do you know the science of it? Do any of you? No. We just try to act as normal as we can and wait. They won't leave us here."

Leave us here? My mind screamed in disbelief. What did that even mean?

Ben and I both looked at each other, the same expression. No need to speak. Our sibling thoughts were in synch.

What was going on?

The counselors were frantic. Sam expressed urgency in evacuating us.

The sheriff acknowledged the concern but didn't seem too worried.

One thing was certain.

Something was about to happen.

But what?

TEN – COLD TRUTH SERVED

And just like that, they tried to make it normal.

"Attention campers," Sam said. "You may leave your cabins and enjoy the activities. Dinner and a special meeting regarding the power outage will be at four this afternoon instead of five. We want to make you aware that, because of the lack of power, there will be no movie tonight. But we look forward to ghost stories around the campfire. Also, important reminder not to eat the ash."

Listening to him ramble on in such a well-acted, everyday fashion, caused me to bob my head as if listening to a song, and roll my eyes at how ridiculous he sounded.

Until he made that comment about the ash.

Was he serious?

Don't eat the ash.

What idiot would actually open their mouth and eat the ash?

"What did I tell you!" I heard Macy outside scolding someone. "Don't eat it."

Scratch that.

I peered out the window to see her playfully smack the arm of one of the boys. I wasn't sure of his name, but he thought it was funny and continued to open his mouth to catch the ash.

"Oh my God," I said.

"Take your turn," Ben stated.

"I'm not sure what this castle thing does."

Ben huffed. "It goes straight or sideways, as many spaces as you want, as they long as no piece is in your way. If it is you can take it."

"Okay, cool." I moved my castle and took one of his pawns.

"Why would you risk your castle like that?"

"I don't know. This is a really dumb game."

"No, it's not. I think you would be really good at it if you tried."

"Ben." I fiddled with one of the pieces. "If something big is going on do you think Mom and George know?"

"Yeah."

"Do you think they'll come?"

Ben looked up at me from the board. "Actually, yeah. I'm surprised they aren't here already."

"Maybe they think they're taking us home."

Ben shrugged.

Just then, the door to my cabin flew open, and Macy barged in. "Marty's brother," she said to Ben. "You're friends with Clarence. Can you tell him not to eat the snow?"

"No, I will not," Ben replied. "If he wants to be stupid enough to eat microscopic glass, then let him. He'll regret it when he's vomiting blood."

"What?" I asked. "Glass?"

Ben did his signature shrug. "Or wood. Or bone, depending on what was being burned. Who knows? It could have been a body."

Macy's face, at that second, was hysterical. She curled her lip above her top teeth, and her mouth dropped open. "Ew-a." She spun and raced back out. "You're eating a dead person!"

Ben didn't flinch. He spoke as he focused on the game board. "Why do girls do that?"

"Do what?"

"Add an A to the end of a word when they're whining, mad, or trying to be dramatic? Like… Ew-a, No-a."

I laughed. "I don't know. I'll make sure I never do it." I moved the horse-shaped piece.

"Good job. Nice move. See? I told you."

"Hey, Ben. Why did you say that?"

"Say what?" Ben made a move.

"About the glass in the ash. What made you say it? Do you know something?"

Ben shook his head. "Nope. I don't. Let's finish this game. We have two hours until we find anything out."

"Okay, sounds good."

Ben moved a piece. "Check mate."

<><><><>

I expected a power-outage-style meal of something cold. Instead, I forgot we were at a camp. The counselors cooked up hotdogs and scrambled eggs over the fire and a large grill. They obviously didn't expect the power to ever come back or else they wouldn't have cooked off the eggs.

Ben was buried in a comic book. So many kids seemed oblivious to anything being wrong. I hoped he wasn't shutting down. Acting like ash falling from the sky was a normal Wyoming thing. Then again, it could be.

Sam stood by the food line and did that stupid "clap three times" to bring silence to the room.

It worked. They were well trained.

"Listen up. Now that everyone is done eating, we need to have a serious discussion," Sam said.

Here it comes, I thought. *Will he tell us the truth, or some grown up laced BS?*

"You all have noticed the lights are out. The power is gone; no WIFI, no cell. And yes, there is a landline, but we have tried to reach someone. We have… a radio." He lifted a finger with an awkward forced smile.

Why was he stalling? It seemed as if he didn't want to get to the point.

The smile dropped, he sucked in his bottom lip, folded his arms and leaned against the food line stand.

"Six minutes exactly... six minutes before that earthquake, I had received an alert from the United States Geological Survey. It said the Yellowstone Caldera was in the early stages of eruption. Now I..." He paused when a wave of voices flowed to him. Lifting his hand to bring silence, Sam continued. "I'll answer your questions after I finish this. Anyhow I... sent a text to Tish, but she didn't see it before the earthquake. Hence, she seemed so upset when she hightailed you out of Lusk. The quake, loss of power, the... ash..." he pointed up. "Are all part of the early stages."

From across the room, another counselor added. "You might want to tell them what a caldera is."

Sam nodded. "Yes. Thank you. A caldera is a volcano."

One of the girls spoke up, "Yellowstone is across the state. Like, five hundred miles from us."

"The volcano," Sam said. "Is what is called a super volcano."

I should have paid more attention when I heard about "super volcanoes," but hearing him say it just sounded so silly. I turned to Ben to ask if it was for real. The seriousness on my brother's face gave me an answer before I even asked.

Suddenly, I needed to know more.

"I radioed the sheriff," Sam told us. "The states are in the process of a massive evacuation. Massive. I mean, the news broke, we are guessing, to the general public. We have one bus; one small bus, and there are a total of seventy people here. The sheriff promised they would get to us and get us out. We have to believe them, and we have to go by what they said. Anyone have any questions?"

I looked around. Were all the other kids so informed about this volcano thing that they didn't have any questions?

After a brief hesitation, I raised my hand. Others did as well.

"John." Sam pointed.

"What about our parents? If they got the warning, wouldn't they come for us?"

"Yes and no," Sam replied. "All roads head east. Doesn't matter which side of the highway. Sheriff said only authorized and emergency vehicles are permitted to go west. It's the only way to get all these people out. So, unless your parents are coming from the west, the best bet is to hang tight here and wait for evacuation. Macy..." he called on her.

"If it's five hundred miles away, we're fine if it erupts. Right?"

Sam shook his head. "I'm not gonna pretend to be an expert. I had six minutes to research before we lost all power. It's a super volcano. I don't know the technical terms; but once it happens, those in what is called the 'kill zone' will die within ten minutes, maybe a little longer, depending how far you are from the volcano. Tens of feet of heavy ash and heat, and deadly gasses. The ash isn't just ash. It's tiny fragments of glass."

When he said that about the ash, I looked at Ben.

Sam continued, "We are ten miles outside the kill zone. Too close for comfort. Honestly, I don't know. I don't want to experience it to find out. I have been trying to get in touch with Clark Westin."

"Who is that?" someone asked.

"A geologist that went off the grid. Everyone around these parts know him as the crazy survival guy. If anyone knows about this stuff, it's him. But I can't get a hold of him on the radio."

I murmured. "He probably evacuated."

Sam heard me. "He probably did."

I raised my hand.

"Marty."

"So, if we aren't out of the campsite and this thing erupts, we're screwed?" I asked.

"In short, yes. We need to get as far east as possible. Everyone does. It's not going to be pretty. People are going to panic. Things will get back. I'm confident. We will be out before it erupts," Sam said.

"How?"

"The sheriff said he would get us."

"And we're supposed to wait?" I asked. "Our parents can't come. What if it goes off tomorrow?"

"It won't. There are experts that study these things." Sam shifted his eyes and pointed. "Ben."

My brother raised his hand. That was odd.

"It is my opinion that we shouldn't chance it," Ben said. "Why take the chance? We need to get out sooner than later, right? So, we get out."

"I understand what you're saying," Sam said. "We can't just walk out."

"Well, we can…" Ben said. "That's not what I am saying. Why are we relying on someone else to save us? We need save ourselves."

"I agree. But we don't have the means."

"We do." Ben pointed to the door. "There's a bus out there."

"It only holds twenty."

"So, you load twenty, maybe a few more on that bus; take the counselors," Ben suggested. "Radio the sheriff. Get authorization. Take the bus to Lusk and get transportation. The counselors you take can drive up to get the rest of us. We make a plan to walk if they don't come back. But we don't wait. I think the sheriff would appreciate you being proactive and that is one less thing on his plate."

I wanted to say, "Wait. Where is my brother?" But I also knew my quiet brother never really spoke like that unless he knew he was right in what he was saying. Ben probably thought hard about his wording, and it showed. He wasn't buried in the comic book, shutting out the world. He was thinking.

Then Ben returned, getting a little nervous. "Sorry, if I sound dumb," Ben said.

"What? No. Not at all." Sam looked at Tish and the others, then back to Ben. "I think it's a great idea, and I can't believe none of us thought of it."

Tish spoke up. "We should leave. It's still early. We should leave now. Radio the sheriff. Make the arrangements."

Sam nodded his agreement. "Who goes? I'll stay behind. You guys find vehicles. Which kids?"

Tish replied. "We can cram the seats. The thirteen- and fourteen-year-olds and the rest of the girls. That should be twenty-five. The counselors can stand and hold on."

Was she really reviving the old "women and children first" rule? "I'm staying with my brother," I said and looked at Ben. "I won't leave him."

"That's fine," Sam replied, then looked at his watch. "I'll try to radio the sheriff. Tish, get everything ready. Just go. No need to take anything."

My brother mumbled something soft. No one but me heard.

He said, "That's not necessarily true."

I faced him. "What? What was that?"

He glanced up from his book to see if anyone was around. "They should take supplies; in case something happens."

"They're only going eight miles."

"Still."

"Hey, Ben," I spoke softly. "How did you know about the ash having glass? I mean it's almost as if you knew it was a volcano."

"I didn't," he said, then flipped to the back of his comic book. He pulled out a map that was folded to be small and handed it to me. "Pops did."

ELEVEN – SLEEEPING ON THE FLOOR

June 16

Sam did as he said. He stayed behind, the lone counselor while the others packed in the small bus with the youngest campers and the rest of the girls.

The plan was for the other counselors to return with enough transportation to get us all out of the camp and to safety.

I was sad that Carla left. But I was also happy. I told her if she made it to Chadron before me and Ben to please find our parents and tell them we were on our way.

We would be… eventually.

Sam let us know they made it to Lusk, and that was just before seven pm, and not long after they left.

Then nothing.

We heard nothing more.

Sam reasoned it was dark, and without any power, the roads would be hard to navigate.

He was confident they'd be back by first light.

Why wouldn't they?

With all the girls gone, I was alone in the cabin. So, I had Ben stay with me.

He was my brother, my big brother. And even though I was the one often protecting him, I needed him with me.

He made me feel safe.

Ben paid attention when no one else did.

He paid attention to Pops.

Pops.

While everyone questioned his state of mind when he stocked the cold cellar and rambled on about his "red-edit" group, Pops was actually the one in the right frame of mind. At least on the apocalypse.

He took the message on the fridge verbatim and in his research, discovered something so compelling to him, he acted on it.

At least for us.

That's what I believed.

When we were in Lusk, I thought about Pops and his June 15 prediction. It had crossed my mind, but quickly slipped from my mind when the earthquake hit.

Why didn't I look in that go bag like my brother did?

I tossed mine in a drawer while Ben opened his.

I thought nothing of it, but Ben thought about it quite a bit.

My cabin was quiet. No teenage girls whispering and giggling. There hadn't been a tremor or earthquake since the one while I was in Lusk. I started to internally calm down some. I went from the mindset of the world is going to end at any second to, "We still have lots of time".

Ben focused on the go bags. He had everything out of them and was organizing the supplies.

The room was lit with an old kerosene lantern. It made me nervous and neurotic worrying it would tip over and catch the room on fire.

After dinner, the only person we spoke to was Sam.

"Get some sleep," Sam told us. "We'll be out of here early. Everything will be alright."

"Do you think they're coming back?" I asked Ben.

"I don't know. They may not be able to or may not find vehicles."

"Wouldn't they tell Sam?"

"They may have already and it's just a front."

I was always a *Titanic* buff. That bit of history fascinated me for some reason. I felt like maybe I was on the *Titanic* and was reincarnated. But hearing my brother imply Sam wasn't being honest made me think of the third-class passengers on the *Titanic*.

How many mothers put their children to bed that fateful April night, telling them everything was going to be alright? Giving them a false comfort to make them not worry.

Was that what Sam was doing to us?

"Marty, go to sleep," Ben told me. "Quit. Okay? It doesn't matter what Sam said. We'll get home."

"How do you know?"

"Because Pops…" he lifted the map. "Figured it out. Look…" He opened the map. "See the circles? He marked the map on where we need to get to and when. We're not in the circle around Yellowstone. We're only close."

"To the kill zone?"

"Yeah. Pops didn't call it that. I think he did this map on the assumption we'd be at camp when it blew."

"So, if we go before it erupts, we'll be fine?" I asked.

"That's what I think."

"But we're basing it on Pops, right?" I questioned. "I mean, how much can Pops know?"

"More than us. Whether he has dementia or not, he was right about this. It doesn't matter that he got it all from Reddit. He was right."

"He put masks in there."

"Yep. For the ash. And he also put in cheaters."

"Cheaters?" I asked.

"Dollar store reading glasses. I guess they were the only eye protection he could think of. They aren't strong so we can still see."

"Maybe we won't need any of this," I said. "I mean, Sam said they're telling him we have time."

"And we might. We have to plan as if we don't."

"Ben, thank you."

"Are you scared, Marty?" he asked.

"Yeah. Wanna know what really scares me? I'm scared that mom and George are gonna come looking for us, and we'll be on our way home, and we'll miss each other."

"Nah." Ben shook his head. "Wanna know what I think? I think we aren't the only ones Pops told the volcano story to. Once Mom and George realize Pops was right and he mapped out our route home, if they do come, that's the route they'll take to us."

"So, we take Pops' route?"

"That's what we do."

"But we won't have to," I said. "The counselors will come back with cars."

"Yeah." Ben didn't sound convincing. "Try to sleep."

"Okay, I'll try. Thanks."

I crawled into the next bed, not far from my brother. I lay there with my eyes closed, trying to sleep. I heard the crinkling of paper and plastic as Ben fiddled with things.

It was one of those time I realized he was the big brother. It was like when we were ten and we stayed at our Aunt Rosa's house. She was old and so was her house. It smelled like moth balls and cat. I hated it, but Ben made it fun.

I loved my brother and hated that people were so mean to him for so long. They treated him horribly, making fun because he was different.

To me, he was never different. He was like all the big brothers my friends had.

Others saw him as quiet and strange. When he focused on something, they called him weird or psycho.

It wasn't fair to him; it was hurtful.

I wish others knew him as I did.

At that moment, as scared as I was, I couldn't imagine being there without Ben. I was glad I had my brother and eventually, the steady noise he made became a white noise and I fell asleep.

<><><><>

"Mart. Marty," Ben called my name.

At first I thought I had only drifted off. Then I realized he was shaking my shoulder. I must have really fallen into a deep sleep.

"Marty."

"Huh?" I rolled over some and squinted. The room was light. "What time is it?"

"It doesn't matter," Ben said. "We have to go. Get dressed. We have to leave."

"Are they back?" I sat up.

"No."

"Aren't we waiting?"

"We can't wait. We don't have time." Ben walked over to the window. "We have to go now."

I swung my legs over the bed, stood, and walked over to join Ben at the window.

Looking out took my breath away.

The falling ash had returned. Only it wasn't like the day before. It wasn't a few flakes drifting down. It was falling steadily and fast.

Outside the cabin, the world was quickly turning gray as the ash began to cover everything.

TWELVE – FIGURE AN OUT

The ceramic mug rattled its way across the table and tumbled to the floor with a crash as the mild earthquake shook the ground.

I felt it in my entire body. Not only the earthquake, but the fear.

"Ben?" I asked with a quivering voice. "Is that it?"

"No. I don't think so. I think something big enough to wipe out a state would sound and feel more intense." Ben stared at an object in his hand.

"What is that?"

He showed me. "A compass. Pops put it in my bag."

"It looks like a toy."

"It works, I think. We'll need it if we lose sight of the road," Ben said. "Head east. Finish up. We have to go."

Finish up.

Ben had told me we needed to take only what we needed. No more than one change of clothes, and we'd fill our bag with more food that we'd take from the dining hall.

Ben had taken the liners from the small trash bins and shoved them in our bags. I didn't know why we would need them.

He thought our journey through, at least as best as he could.

Pops had provided face masks and glasses; and Ben came up with the idea that the rain ponchos would provide extra protection. We'd wear them over our clothes and backpacks.

I was certain we looked ridiculous, draped in those too big, bright red, cheap plastic ponchos. They were so big we tied the waists with bath towels Ben had cut up.

At least we'd stick out in the gray ash.

Clothed and packed, Ben opened the door, and we walked out.

Across the courtyard, I saw several of the teenage boys on the porch of the cabins. Looking out at the ash in wonder.

"Where are you going?" one asked.

"Leaving." Ben replied.

"Are they back?" he asked the same question I did.

"Nope." Ben shook his head.

"You shouldn't go. You should wait."

Ben paused walking. "There's no time."

"You're gonna kill your sister taking her out in this!"

Now I was the one who stopped. "Shut up!" I blasted him. "He's saving me."

Ben tugged my arm, talking through clenched jaws. "That's a little melodramatic. Let's just grab some stuff from the dining hall."

For as gray as it was, I expected it to be cool. It wasn't. Although I was certain the temperature would drop with the sun being clouded over.

The ash wasn't slippery or deep; a dusting over the grass and walkways. It crunched beneath my feet.

We made it to the dining hall, stomping our feet to clear the ash before going in.

"We need gloves," Ben said. "We'll take the rubber ones from the kitchen."

"What do we need gloves for?"

"We need to protect our skin from the ash. And try not to talk. We don't want to breathe it in."

"How do you know so much?"

"I don't." He shook his head. "I really don't. Just common sense." He led the way to the back. "Grab water. I'm gonna get what I can."

The water bottles were out on the big silver table. As I reached for them, placing a few in my bag, next to the case, I saw a knife. It was probably used to open the plastic on the water. Thinking about it, I put that knife in the front pocket of my bag. Feeling like it was a crime, I turned my head to see if my brother saw me take the knife. But he was busy shoving a box of latex gloves in his bag.

"What are you doing?" Sam's voice entered the kitchen.

I was startled and turned. "We're... we're leaving."

"Walking?" Sam asked.

"Yes." I nodded.

"Ben. You can't take your sister out in this," Sam said. "You should wait."

"We can't wait, Sam," Ben said. "It's coming down. I don't want to take a chance."

"They said there's time."

I asked, "Who said? When was this? Did you talk to them today?"

Sam went silent.

"Sam," I said. "Don't stay. What if they don't come back? You'll be stuck here." I zipped up my bag and put it over my back. It was heavier, a lot heavier with the water. "You said it's not safe here."

"Marty it's safer than out there. They'll be back. I can't let you guys leave," Sam told us.

Ben stepped forward. "We can't stay." He fixed my poncho over my backpack. "We have to leave now. You should think about it. We only need to make it to the main road. We probably could get a ride."

"Or get hit by a car that doesn't see you."

I laughed. "In these ponchos?"

Sam shook his head. "They'll be covered in ash, and you'll blend in before long. It's foolish and dangerous. Do you see it out there?" Sam asked. "It's coming down fast."

"Exactly. Which tells me we don't have much more time." My brother faced me. "You ready?"

I nodded.

"Let's do this."

Sam stood by the door. He asked us once more not to go. He did so with sincerity and concern. Then once he realized he couldn't stop us, he wished us luck.

And we stepped out. Out of the kitchen and out of the building.

It was time to go.

I wasn't sure if it was right or wrong. It was something we had to do.

There was no choice.

What did we know? Really nothing.

Going on what we thought, common sense, and hope.

No scientific knowledge to fall back on. No source of news or information.

Venturing out blindly with a compass from a cereal box and makeshift protective clothing.

We were venturing out into a world that was already deadly, with an even bigger danger on the horizon. Worst of all, we were doing it alone.

THIRTEEN – HEYMAN ROAD

The route to the main road had slight inclines and turns. It was still a straight shot to the main road below. A road, if Sam was correct, was only going east.

According to Pops' map, it was the road we were to take. Eighty-six miles straight on that one highway. A secondary highway, two lanes wide, and if what we learned was correct, all traffic was headed east on that road.

The way we needed to go.

For sure, someone would see us. Two kids walking the road. They'd offer us a ride.

Wouldn't they?

It was a six-mile walk down that road, and it would take us hours to accomplish.

Our pace was steady but slow.

I didn't want to breathe heavy or talk for fear that the ash would get into my lungs.

Ben went silent. I supposed it was his way to keep his mouth shut... literally.

It was a strange sensation once we left the dining hall and trekked across the camp to the main entrance. I felt isolated and alone, even though my brother was with me.

Ben was to my left, two paces ahead of me.

We walked in silence.

Every inch of my body, with the exception of my cheeks, was covered. Even they had been shielded some by the hood of my red poncho.

It looked like it should have been cold, but it wasn't. Not yet.

Barely a mile into the walk, I could feel the heat building.

It was warm; muggy almost. I started to sweat and wanted to rip off the layers of clothes, but I knew I couldn't.

A part of me felt as if I were suffocating. It wasn't the ash; it was how I was dressed.

My mouth covered; eyes blocked. The hood caused a tunnel vision effect, blocking out everything in my peripheral vision as the plastic crinkled loudly against my ears.

Crinkle. Crinkle. Crinkle.

Even if Ben did speak to me, I wouldn't hear him.

I imagined, with the exception of the heat, that it was how it felt walking in the snow.

A deafening silence brought on by the sound-muffling ash, the crunch of my feet with each step I took, and the blocked sound of my hearing.

We kept moving.

Once in a while, Ben would stop, look back, and give me a look as if to ask if I were okay.

I'd nod, he'd turn and walk again.

I followed his lead, putting my trust in my brother, and quietly walked behind him.

A lot of thoughts passed through my mind in that silent journey to the main road.

My mother.

Was she listening to the news, freaking out, worried about us?

Did she insist that George leave to come get us?

No, she didn't. She wouldn't need to.

George loved us.

I imagined he wouldn't hesitate to get in his truck to get us. He probably hit a roadblock, unable to get through.

My baby sister Ruby would be clueless. But my family wouldn't be immune to the effects.

They weren't that far away. A hundred miles from where Ben

and I were.

In the scheme of things with a super volcano, I imagined a hundred miles was nothing.

Were they looking out the window seeing the ash?

And Pops.

With the storm cellar packed, Pops probably stood in the kitchen, pointing to the sign on the fridge, saying, "See, I told you so. I told you. That Red-Edit group was right. Let's go get those kids."

Pointing to the map and telling George, "This is the way I told them to go. Let's take the truck and find them."

I had known Pops since I was not much older than Ruby.

I knew what my mother and George said about him having dementia, but I didn't see it. Maybe it was my age or that I didn't want to see it.

Pops was still the same.

There was no way he had dementia. He was too strong, too smart. And I was certain he was out there looking for us.

He'd find us, or we'd find him.

I believed that. I really did.

FOURTEEN – LONE RESCUER

Halfway down Heyman road, Ben stopped to shake his poncho. It wasn't completely covered like Sam had suggested. Jut a thin layer rested on his shoulders and hood. I did the same and continued walking.

By the time we reached the end of the campsite road, the falling ash slowed down.

I imagined Sam was thinking we were idiots for not waiting. But it wasn't just a passing thing. The falling ash was the beginning to something unstoppable.

It took us hours to walk the six miles down Heyman, which in turn, took us to another secondary road. By my estimate, it was another mile, not long until we arrived at Route Twenty, the highway that would take us straight home. The road Pops said for us to stay on.

Two cars passed us as we walked that road. Not the massive evacuation I expected it to be, but then we heard the highway before we even saw it.

Horns beeping and blaring. Everyone honking at each other to move quickly. Move to where? It was jammed; but at least it was moving. Slowly, but moving forward.

More miles of cars than there were miles of highway or maybe an accident. Ben and I would find out before those in the cars did. We actually moved at a slightly faster pace, and we weren't the only ones.

So many people walked.

It wasn't hundreds, but it was more than just Ben and I. Everyone stayed a little bit of distance from each other. But we all walked on the other side of the guardrail.

There was a family behind us. I wondered why they were walking.

Then I saw two people get out of a car.

That was the issue. People were leaving their cars and deciding to walk, causing the traffic to back up more.

It was one of those situations of act now, go east, and think later. Did they even know where they would go or how far they would have to walk?

At least Ben and I had an end game.

I started to get tired from all the walking. My feet hurt. I was hot and sweaty. That poncho was the reason It was so warm. The uneven ground didn't help my aching legs either.

My lips were dry under my mask. I needed a drink of water, but I was fearful pulling out my bottle. What if someone took it?

"Ben," I caught up to him. "We need to stop soon."

"I know. We will. Next building or place we see, we'll stop. Okay."

I don't know why, but suddenly, I started getting worried. There was a sense of being vulnerable. We were young; all by ourselves in a world that could explode at any second.

Even though the ash had stopped falling, there was a haze around everything. The cars moving on the ash and the people walking dusted it up. It was hard to see more than ten feet in front of me. I walked fast to keep up to Ben. I didn't want to lose him.

It reminded me of the time in a haunted house. The fog was thick. Like the haunted house, I was waiting for something to jump out at me.

It was hard to gauge distance. I realized that when it seemed the flashing police lights were only a few feet away. But they weren't, they were just reflecting in the haze.

When we finally arrived at the police car, there was no officer. Just the squad car with the flashing lights.

How far had we walked? I felt as if we had been walking forever. My legs hurt even more. My stomach twisted in hunger, and my throat felt scratchy and dry.

I had been holding my water bottle under my poncho. I stopped, lifted my mask, and took a drink. I had to. I quickly hid it again.

"You alright?" Ben asked.

"Getting tired. Do you know how far we've walked?"

"Since this road? Three miles."

"Three miles? That's it?"

"That's close to eleven miles already. We're ten percent there."

My brother picked that moment to be optimistic? I was wearing down, and it was still early.

A feeling of defeat and regret started pounding at me.

Then I heard something that changed everything at that moment.

A series of "blings" came from Ben's phone, and "bloops" from mine. My phone sounded more muffled.

We had walked into a signal.

Our phones were sending alerts for texts, voicemails, or both.

Both of us stopped.

"That's our phones," I said excitedly.

Ben's was easier for him to retrieve than mine. He reached into his pocket. Me, I had to swing around my backpack and get the phone from the side pocket. I glanced up to see Ben staring at his phone.

"From mom. Texts and missed calls," he replied, then immediately tried to call.

I looked down at my texts. George had sent seven.

"Nothing," Ben said. "It's not connecting."

"George is asking if we're okay," I told him.

"Mom, too. She wants us to get back."

My fingers moved quickly, replying to George that we were fine and on our way home on foot.

Please reply. Please reply.

Bloop.

I sighed out.

"Roads are all closed going west. We tried to drive there," George texted.

A few seconds later, in the midst of my reply...

Bloop.

"Calls won't go through."

"What's he saying?" Ben asked.

"Roads are closed. They tried to come and can't get through by calling."

"Tell him we're on our way. We'll stay in touch as much as we can."

I nodded and continued my text. That we were safe, on our way and taking the route that Pops mapped out.

Bloop.

When I saw the text, my heart dropped. "Oh my God."

"What?" Ben asked. "What is it?"

I handed Ben the phone.

"Good, stay the course. Keep an eye out for Pops," George replied. "He left yesterday for you on horseback."

FIFTEEN – GOING WESTIN

Midway Tool Company wasn't a hardware store, like I thought. Not sure why I thought it was. Maybe it was the name. It certainly didn't look like a store from the outside.

It was a small, metal looking office building with a couple windows right off the road.

It was a good place to stop and take a break. An overdue break.

The door was open, and we shook off the ash before we walked in, leaving our ponchos by the door.

I wanted badly to take off my shoes, but I didn't. There was a reception area that looked like a doctor's office, with couches and chairs, and it was a perfect spot to plop down and rest.

It was darker in there and not as warm as outside.

It was nearly three o'clock. No wonder I was hungry.

"Just a snack," Ben said. "We'll save our food for when we stop for the night."

"Okay." I reached in my pack and pulled out one of those little bags of cereal.

I tried to call George and my mom again. Nothing. I even sent a text that we were taking a break. It had been over an hour since I heard from him. He had sent us a long text with things he learned.

"And last," the text read. "They are saying it won't happen yet, but if it blows while you're on your way, take cover. You will have about thirty minutes until the ash cloud comes."

When I had read that text to Ben, he replied that it was called a pyro something cloud.

"They move seven hundred miles an hour," Ben said. "Yeah, that makes sense."

He studied the map Pops gave him. A tourist map of Highway Twenty, marking all the stops along what was known as the oldest and longest highway in the United States.

Probably something Pops grabbed at Walmart.

Mine was a normal map. Well, not normal. Pops had taken pages out of an atlas and taped them together.

My heart ached when I thought of Pops.

George didn't convey that he was too overly concerned, but I knew he was. He truly believed Pops was "slipping". To have his seventy-four-year-old father on horseback in the middle of a super volcano eruption was scary enough. But to think he could get confused, lost, or hurt was frightening.

What made it worse, what made me feel awful, was that Pops left looking for us.

We just had to stay the route, be vigilant, keep an eye out, and hope he was alright.

Maybe he turned around and went back home, and we just hadn't heard.

I was careful as I dumped my cereal into my mouth. I didn't want any ash on it.

"So… here we are," Ben showed me the tourist map. "Obviously, the tool company isn't on here. But in another two miles, there looks like a bunch of different stuff is coming up. Two miles. We can do that before sundown. I'll keep checking the map. We'll push it till we reach that area."

"How long will it take us?" I asked.

"I hope we can get a ride once we get past the traffic. Right now, it won't do us any good. We're making faster time. We aren't walking fast because we don't want to get winded."

"So, it will take us days?"

"Two more. I estimate us to be walking three miles an hour. Has to be. We left at ten, we've walked fifteen miles. So, at that pace, we can do this. We have to stay the route."

"Pops."

"Pops, yep. I wonder how he thought he was going to help us both on one horse?"

I shrugged. "Maybe just being with us. Watching over us."

"I hope he's okay."

"Me…" I heard the door open, and for a split second, I thought for sure it was Pops.

Then I looked.

It wasn't him. It was a younger man. He had a scarf tied around his mouth and nose. He wore a jean jacket and was coated with ash.

At first, it appeared he was just another traveler. A weary walker, getting out of the ash, taking a break.

He just stared at us.

Ben said, "Hey," an acknowledgement and returned to showing me the map.

The man stepped closer.

He wasn't alone, another man stood in the doorway. That one was a little older.

"What do you have?" the man asked.

"A map," I answered.

"You got food? Water?" the man asked.

Ben didn't answer.

I started to get nervous.

"Hey!" he yelled. "What's in the bags? I'm talking to you."

"Our stuff," I replied. "Just our stuff. We're just trying to get home."

"Marty," Ben spoke through clenched teeth.

Then the man pulled out a pistol. He extended it and pointed it at us. "Give me your bags."

The man at the door walked inside. He held a rifle.

"Give me your stuff now," the Jean Jacket Man demanded. "Nothing is stopping me from shooting you."

"Is that right," the older man behind him said. Before I realized it, he had the rifle against the younger man's head. "You're not shooting anyone. Hand it over."

Jean Jacket Man didn't budge, and the older man took the pistol from his hand.

"Get out now. Now," the older man warned. "If I see you on the road, I will shoot you."

The younger man backed up, spun, and took off.

"That was easier than I thought," the man said. He examined the gun. I wasn't sure what he was doing with it. He moved something on it, then handed it to me. "There's not one in the chamber. And this here." He showed me. "Is the safety. It's on. You wanna use it, turn it off. It's loaded. Don't shoot me."

I just looked at it.

"Take it," he said. "You may need it."

Ben reached up and took the gun. "Thank you, sir. Thank you for coming in here."

"Well, I was looking for you. Are you the Lowe siblings?"

I nodded. "We are."

"Heard on my radio that you guys took off on foot. From the camp. I was already on the road. Been keeping an eye out. I knew when I saw those red ponchos, it was you. I watched you walk in here; and when I saw that guy follow, I knew he was trouble. I, of course, was sitting in that traffic out there."

"Sam?" I asked. "You spoke to Sam?"

He shook his head. "I listened to Sam. He's worried. I think they may be getting out of there soon. Last I monitored, they were talking to the sheriff. You guys got a good head start." He backed up. "Did you want a ride? I have room in my truck."

I looked at Ben.

Ben shook his head. "No, thank you. We learned our grandfather left on horseback to look for us. He's taking this road."

"Horseback huh? I'll keep an eye out for him and let him know I saw you."

"Thank you," Ben said. "Maybe if we run into you down the road we'll change our minds, but right now, walking is faster."

He chuckled. "That's a good point. You're moving as fast as I am right now."

"Who are you?" I asked.

"Clark. Clark Westin."

"Ah," I said. "Yeah, you're that survival guy Sam talked about."

"Not much of one if I'm stuck in traffic." He winked. "And you're sure you don't want a ride."

Both Ben and I shook our heads.

"Okay. Well, be careful. And don't use that gun on each other when you have some sort of sibling fight."

"We won't," Ben replied.

I knew my brother took him literally. He didn't often get sarcasm.

"Be careful. And if you see she erupts, take cover... fast."

Then just like that, Clark Westin walked out.

He came, saved us, gave advice, and left.

I barely had time to register what he looked like. I wasn't sure if I'd recognize him again.

I was far too nervous to pay attention. Especially with the other guy pointing the gun at us and thinking Clark was with him.

It all happened so fast. I was reeling in the aftermath. Trying to calm down.

My brother didn't look fazed. Not even when the guy pointed his gun at us and asked for our stuff. And not when Clark stopped it all.

Clark left. And just like the feeling I had over Pops, a part of me knew we'd see him again.

There wasn't time to think more about it. Ben gathered up his stuff.

Break was over. It was time to go.

SIXTEEN – DUCK AND COVER

The next leg of the walk was easier. I know I felt refreshed. And not long after we left, I started to forget about the man who tried to rob us. Although it didn't stop me from looking over my shoulder.

When we left the Midway Tool Company, Clark hadn't made much progress. He was in his truck. He did this whistle thing to get our attention and waved. His truck was an old green color, and he was six or so cars back from the turn to the tool store.

It was funny. Every so often he'd pass us, and then we'd pass him.

Almost a game that made the time go faster.

"Look, there's Clark," Ben would say.

Then we'd pick up the pace.

Each time we walked by him, which seemed to be two or three times a mile, I got a better look at him.

Once my mother made me watch a really dated movie about a Crocodile Hunter from Australia. For some reason, Clark reminded me of him. A worn face with folds of skin and wrinkles that came from smiling a lot. He wore a hat, but I could see his graying, blonde hair that was just a bit too long for a man nearly Pops age.

He was cool though.

He saved us.

Traffic broke free and cars suddenly picked up their pace. Clark beeped and waved arrogantly at us.

"He's gonna get way ahead this time," I said.

"Eventually, we'll catch him."

"Maybe. I mean any idea when we'll stop?"

"There's a diner…" Ben showed me the map. "Like a replica of an old diner. That's what the map says. It's about two miles ahead. It might be too early to stop. But the next thing on the map is four miles past that. It'll be too dark."

"Maybe there are buildings like the tool company."

"I don't want to chance it. We'll stop there. That will put us at twenty-four miles for the day."

"That's crazy."

"I know, right?" Ben said.

"Maybe Pops is close. He left yesterday."

Ben didn't say anything.

"Where do you think Pops is now?" I asked.

Ben shrugged.

"He has to be near us. Right, Ben?"

"If he's okay."

"What do you mean?"

"He's not okay normally, Marty. You know that."

"No, I don't." I shook my head. "I refuse to believe that."

"That's because you haven't seen it. This whole end-of-the-world thing was a fluke for him."

"Fluke? Where did you learn that word?" I asked.

"Marty, he's not well. It's scary to think he's out here alone. I don't want him hurt or sick or lost," Ben said. "He's the only grandfather we've known."

"No, Ben. He's okay. I think it's just him being old."

"He's not that old."

I chuckled. "Please."

"Marty there have been presidents older than him."

"Still …"

"No, Marty. Did you know…" Ben stopped talking.

I waited, assuming he was thinking of the right words.

"Ben? What?"

"Nothing."

"What?"

"You know what happened that made us come out here, right?"

"They said Pops needed help on the farm."

"Ranch," Ben corrected. "His workers were saying he was slipping. Forgetting things. The accountant had to take over the orders."

"Oh." I waved out my hand. "I knew that stuff."

"Did you know he went into town looking for George?"

"Okay."

"But it wasn't so much looking for George recently. He was insistent that George was a teenager and Pops had no idea what was going on or even when it was. I guess the pastor of the church found him and stayed with him, until George could get out here."

A lump formed in my throat. "That makes me really sad."

"It makes me upset to think Pops is out here alone."

"He's been pretty normal," I said. "Maybe he won't have an episode."

"Let's hope."

Ben said that, and I think he believed it. But in our walk, we became too comfortable; in a stride, not paying attention to what was happening around us.

Not… looking back.

Had we done so, we would have seen him coming.

The Jean Jacket Man from the Midway Tool Company.

The one that tried to rob us.

I don't know where he came from: a car or walking. Maybe he followed and waited for Clark to get ahead of us.

I didn't know.

But by the time I saw him, he was a blur. Like some sort of football player or professional wrestler, he slammed, shoulder first, into my unsuspecting brother.

The man hit my teenage brother, and the force of the hit, not only knocked my brother down, it sent him sailing and rolling down the slight grade before he came to a stop.

I don't think Jean Jacket Man expected my brother to get so far ahead. He charged for my brother, his feet slipping in the ash.

"Get up, Ben! Get up! Run!"

I could see that Ben had the wind knocked out of him. As he tried to get up, he looked confused. But he wasn't up for long.

Just as he made it to his hands and knees, Jean Jacket Man kicked him, flipping him over.

"No!" I screamed and ran. But I was weighted down by a heavy backpack.

My heart hurt so bad for my brother as I watched the man dive for him.

"Leave him alone! Just take what you want!" I cried out as I ran over. In my mind, all I saw was those videos online where people get jumped. People don't fight fair. They stop when someone is down. Men cheat and get mean when they fight, losing all reason. That's what I had seen. They cheat and kick and stomp heads, and I was so scared he was going to do that to my brother.

I had to do something.

I took off my bag, dropping it to the ground. And I jumped on Jean Jacket Man.

"Leave him alone!" My fist pummeled him. "Get off my brother!"

It stopped him, but it didn't really work. He turned around and shoved me. Down I went, and I landed by my backpack.

I had to stop him. I had to. It was my brother.

As I got up to try again, looking for a rock or something, I remembered.

Hurriedly, I grabbed for my backpack, unzipped the front, reached in, and pulled out the knife I had taken from camp.

I was smart enough to know it was a chance. He could turn it on me, but I had to help Ben.

Blood rushed to my ears. I heard my own heartbeat, and things moved in a violent slow motion. Then with everything I had, all of my weight, pointed end out, I lunged for Jean Jacket Man as he hovered over my brother. I wasn't aiming the knife. I just wanted to land it somewhere, and I did.

The knife plunged into the back of his neck, missing the bone.

He stopped and lifted his head.

I was on his back, and I locked my legs around him. He wasn't going to throw me off again.

He wasn't dead. He wasn't down, and he wasn't stopping.

Pulling out the knife was harder than stabbing him. I only got it out a little, and I pushed it back it.

I wasn't sure why, but when I pulled back the second time, the knife came out easily. And with it, so much blood.

He tried to stand, but I wasn't letting go. He was hunched over from the weight of my body, and I plunged the knife in him again.

He hurt my brother.

I stabbed him again.

I could see Ben not moving.

I stabbed him again.

"You hurt my brother!"

Another stab.

All in the neck.

Go down. Go down. Go down! I screamed in my mind. With each plunge of the knife, it fueled such a hatred I had never felt before.

Then, finally, he toppled over, with me landing on top of him. The second he hit the ground, I released the knife, jumped up, and ran to Ben.

I muttered his name fast, over and over as I dropped down next to him. "Ben. Ben. Ben! Please get up. Please be alive."

I could feel it. My throat swelling up; my eyes watering. I was on the verge of sobbing. My brother lay on his side, his face covered with abrasions.

"Ben, please," I whimpered.

His eyelids fluttered, and then he opened his eyes.

"Oh my God," I gasped and hugged him. "Oh my God. Are you okay?"

"I think so," he said weakly.

I helped him sit up. His cheater glasses were broken, and I removed them from his face. "What hurts?" I asked.

"My head, nose. My ribs, but…" He lifted the poncho, exposing a smaller bag he carried in front. "I think my packs took the brunt."

I reached for his water bottle on the side of his pack and removed his mask. "Tilt your head back. I want to get some of this ash off your face."

He tilted back his head, and I slowly poured the water on him.

He winced.

"Can you stand?" I asked. "We'll move slow. We'll get to the diner and finish getting you cleaned up. Maybe we'll see Clark."

Ben nodded, and with my help, started to stand. But he stopped and plopped back down. His eyes widened, and I thought for sure Jean Jacket Man was coming. Until Ben slowly looked at me with this horror on his face. "Marty? What… what happened? Did you do that?"

Then it hit me. Jean Jacket Man wasn't coming for us. The extent of what I did never registered until I looked back over my shoulder and saw him.

He lay in a huge puddle of his own blood, my knife next to his head which was nearly severed from his body.

Instantly I got sick.

What little I did eat just shot from my stomach and into my mouth.

I scurried away from Ben and on hands and knees. I threw up. It wasn't much, but my stomach kept wanting to twist and turn.

I sickened myself.

What had I done?

I knew I was trying to help my brother. But I took a life, and I did so brutally.

"Marty." Ben put his hand on my back.

"I'm sorry, Ben. I'm sorry," I started crying. "I'm sorry."

"It's okay."

"How… how can say that?"

"He would have killed me, Marty. I would have done the same thing."

My shoulders bounced as I cried, staring at the smelly pile of vomit mixed with ash.

I was ready to say something. What that was, I don't recall, because the ground suddenly shook violently.

The sounds of blaring car horns and alarms carried to us. And as Ben helped me to my feet, we both stopped cold.

When I saw it, I couldn't move. I was terrified. The entire western horizon looked as if it were on fire. The bright orange made its way through every crevice and break in the dark clouds, making them appear like smoke lingering above an inferno.

Boom. Boom. Boom. Boom.

It wasn't just one, it was four. Though in the distance, I knew if I could hear the explosions as they shattered the earth hundreds of miles away, I shuddered to think how massive the eruption truly was.

"Marty, we have to go. We have to go now." Ben took hold of my arm, pulling me as he looked at the sky. "We have thirty minutes."

SEVENTEEN – THE HIP PLACE

Time check: four-fourteen. When Ben said we had thirty minutes, I knew that was an estimate.

I aimed for shelter in twenty.

There were several things that happened following the eruption. Realizations.

I knew the so-called "experts" were all wrong; that Yellowstone wasn't days or weeks away from erupting. The reports of "there is time" were mainly to keep calm.

My gut told me it was going to erupt while we were out and about.

I didn't expect to have to move quickly, to race against the clock to get shelter.

There was still a chance that we would be fine. That the "pyroclastic cloud," as Ben called it, would break before it hit us.

It all depended on how big the eruption was.

If it was smaller, then the cloud wouldn't make it to us.

We knew nothing.

The cloud thing was it. We knew that was a possibility. What happened after the eruption was a mystery to us. We had been away, locked up in an informational prison. We had never educated ourselves enough. Would the ash keep falling, or was it an instant dump?

I knew I had to focus on getting to shelter.

Ben was hurt. He tried to hide it, but I could tell by how he moved that every step hurt him.

The plan to get to shelter and get him cleaned up was out the window and replaced with a run-and-hide tactic.

The diner wasn't far. I just hoped something else came up along the way in case we needed it.

The eruption was a starting gun to some massive great race to who could panic the fastest.

I tried to put Jean Jacket Man out of my mind, and in the rush to get to safety, somehow I managed. But I knew it wouldn't stay tucked away forever.

The attack from Jean Jacket Man threw us about a hundred feet from the highway.

We were safe and didn't realize it until we tried to rush to the road.

As we made it closer to the road, we heard the honking, the sound of metal against metal.

It was suddenly every man for himself as those jam-packed cars tried to break free somehow and go east.

One would think someone would see two kids and try to help.

No.

We stayed back, watching the drivers of the cars go insane.

Back up, hit a car.

Turn the wheel, hit another car.

Smash and crash with no regards at all to get free of the congestion somehow.

The patience of waiting in the slow-moving exodus was gone.

I watched a car drive to the side of the road and run against the guardrail, sparks flying as they tried to get ahead.

Other cars followed, only to be cut off.

It was as if they knew the ash cloud of death was coming, and it was run for the hills.

They abandoned their cars, opting to go on foot.

The highway fast became impassible. One long trainwreck of cars.

I wondered if that was the safest bet.

What would they do once the cloud passed? Go back to their car?

They were suddenly like me and Ben. On foot, running forward.

Ben and I weren't running.

He couldn't.

Ben hobbled. We held onto each other and moved as quickly as we could.

I knew the diner wasn't that far; that even at a slower pace, we would make it.

Ben needed medical attention. His nose was busted up, and he bled pretty bad from his temple.

I kept looking for Clark.

Was he really that far ahead?

I hoped we could find shelter. We aimed for the diner, but anywhere in-between would work. I hoped.

Then I spotted a building. I knew it couldn't be the diner. It didn't look like one, but it was bigger.

I could see people running to it, all those ahead of us that moved faster. People moving alone or with families. All racing toward that long building. It would be safe. Safer than the tool building because it was brick.

Hopefully, when the ash cloud came, it wouldn't destroy the buildings.

The closer we got, I saw it was a veterinarian clinic, and that made me happy.

"Ben, look," I said. "Bet we can get stuff in there to clean your cuts."

"How many windows? It's hard for me to see."

My brother's eyes were swollen and grew worse by the minute. "Not many," I replied.

"We just need to get away from windows, that's all."

It was the place to go. I watched someone go in, and no one else seemed to be headed that way.

I picked up the pace, holding onto my brother as we made it to the door.

It was a single glass door with the hours of operation on it.
I reached for it and pulled.
Locked.
How was it locked? All those people were inside?
I pulled again, no luck.
Thinking maybe they were being cautious against people like Jean Jacket Man, I knocked and knocked.
"Hey! Help us! Let us in! Please!" I peeked in and saw it was crammed, packed with people. It was where the people on the highway had taken shelter.
A man walked over to door. "Sorry. We can't. We have too many."
His voice was muffled, but I could understand what he said.
"No! My brother needs help."
"Marty. Let's go. The diner."
I pounded on the door. "Open up, please!"
He shook his head and walked away.
I growled out a scream in frustration.
"It can't be far, Marty. Let's head for the diner."
"What if it's the same? What if people locked that door?"
"Then we'll hope a car is safe. Let's go."
I looked back at the door and to the man who had his back to us. How could they do that? How could they just refuse to let us in?
We had to move forward and keep going.
Time check: four-thirty-five
Twenty-one minutes had passed since I started the timing.
I begged out loud and silently for us to make it.
There was a huge chance that whatever was coming our way was nothing deadly. That only the heavy ash would come, falling like a snowstorm and giving us time to get out.
But we didn't know.
We knew nothing.
We had to go on the assumption of worst-case scenario, and we moved faster in those last moments than we had moved since we left the camp.

There was urgency, and Ben put aside his injuries to give it everything he had.

Traffic moved some on the road, but cars still drove erratically, crashing and honking. There was so much rushing and chaos, the movement of the people and cars caused a dust-up of the ash, causing a thicker haze.

Voices carried through the clouds of ash.

Women and men shouting out things, children crying.

Then I saw it.

The diner.

There was no way/no how it was safe.

A throwback and relic of days gone by, the long metal tubular building was our last hope of shelter, and it wasn't even that much at all.

It had so many windows.

As we approached the door, I could see people inside and braced myself to be turned away.

Were there cars we could run to? A truck, maybe? I checked what was close.

Then a vibration began.

A gentle vibration beneath our feet.

Whatever would hit us… we were out of time.

As I reached for the door, my brother at my side, a woman opened it.

"Hurry," she said, then pulled at me. "Get inside." She wore a light blue shawl over her head. It was covered with a light gray film. It was probably her protection from the ash when she was outside.

"Are you alright?" she asked.

I nodded and exhaled heavily in relief as Ben and I made it into the diner.

There were so many people standing around, looking scared and as confused as I felt.

The vibration grew stronger.

"Stay clear of the windows!" someone shouted.

The woman pulled us farther in.

It didn't feel like an earthquake. It was a strange rumbling that grew stronger by the second. For some reason, the earthquake drills we used to have kicked in, and I spun to Ben.

"We need to get under something," I told Ben.

"Table," he replied, then looked around. "A booth."

There were many to choose from. They lined the walls of the diner

Ben took the lead, grabbing my hand, and dragged me to a corner booth. "Under the table," he ordered.

It was a tight squeeze. Even though we were thick with our backpacks and supplies, we quickly crawled under the table.

It was like the little tents we made when we were kids. We'd play camping in our room, building a fortress of blankets and toys.

Protected and safe from the world.

We crouched under that table, our backs near the wall as the booth seats crowded us in on both sides.

The rumbling grew stronger and louder. A pressure built in my ears, and instinctively, I placed my hands over them, tensing my body. Cowering even more under the shelter of that table.

I lifted my eyes to see the woman with the blue shawl. She had crouched down at the end of the table.

She said something. Her mouth was moving, hand reaching out. She had a gentle face and was trying to get us. Perhaps calm us because she knew we were scared.

I was scared.

I couldn't hear her.

What was she saying? I shook my head as it built.

I can't hear you. I don't understand you.

The energy intensified. The vibration increased to the point that I felt it in every inch of my body.

Louder.

Louder.

My eyes were focused on the woman.

I saw her glance upward, only for a second.

With what seemed a popping release of pressure, even with

my ears covered, I heard the windows in the diner all shatter at the same time.

There were screams, lots of them.

And a black thickness poured in through the windows. Flood waters made of a thick cloud of ash.

It encompassed everything and everyone, even the woman in the blue shawl.

Swallowing it all, consuming every bit of light until everything was dark and I could see nothing.

Then it was quiet.

EIGHTEEN – ANYONE THERE?

It never got light. Only quiet.

At least for the first few minutes.

Under that table, protected by the wall behind us and the booth benches, Ben and I huddled.

Had anyone else climbed under a table? Had they made it safely?

I heard no one. Not a cough, sniffle, or cry.

"Ben," I said his name softly.

"Don't talk much. Keep your mouth covered."

"Are you okay?" I asked.

"Yeah, you?'

"I fine. Should we leave?"

"No. Not yet."

I felt my brother shuffle a bit next to me. Then, the tiny light from his watch lit up his face. He shook his head. "We'll stay. Try to rest."

I couldn't see anything, not a foot in front of my face. Ben's watch lighting up was the only time I saw anything.

It was a strange event. Not once did I lose consciousness. I heard every window explode, the wall behind us vibrate. I heard every scream go from strong to muffled.

How much ash had fallen? How far east had it spread?

I hated not knowing anything at all. What would we be walking into? Surely the ash didn't reach our home.

I hoped not. All I thought about under that table was my

family. My mother and George so worried. Little Ruby not having a clue what was going on. And on top of fearing for me and Ben, they had to be worried about Pops.

And I was getting really hungry. I'd hold off eating as long as possible. It couldn't be healthy eating ash-covered food.

"Ben?"

"Yeah."

"Do you think we're the only ones who made it?"

Before Ben could answer, a voice called out in the darkness. A male voice.

"No. I'm alive. I'm under a table."

"Me too," someone else said.

A third voice commented. "I saw someone run in the freezer."

A conversation between them entailed in the dark.

"Should we go?" asked one.

"Not yet. Let's wait. Hopefully, by morning there will be some light."

"Anyone have a flashlight?"

"I do," the man replied. "I'm not using it yet. Unless I need it. We may need it to get out in the morning."

A flashlight was one thing Pops packed in our go bags. It wasn't a big flashlight. In fact, it was little and ran on double-A batteries. It was on a keychain, hooked to my backpack. I hoped it worked.

Ben said his injuries weren't hurting him. I didn't see how that was. Then again, we weren't moving.

After the ash cloud hit us, it was warm, uncomfortably warm. I was crammed next to my brother, and his body heat with the red plastic ponchos made it unbearable.

That was at first.

Then the hours ticked on.

It started to get cold. The temperature dropped steadily, and my hands started to hurt. The skin was tight from the dry air.

I asked Ben if he was hungry, and he said he wasn't. He was fine sipping his water.

My mouth was so dry, and my lips cracked, and it hurt to move them. I hadn't even taken my water bottle out.

It was time. I'd grab a granola bar as well.

"I'm sorry," I said to Ben as I shuffled to get my backpack.

"It's okay. What are you doing?"

"Getting my bag. I need water, and I'm hungry."

Blindly I felt my bag and the zipper. I knew where everything was. Feeling for the water bottle was easy. I pulled that out and rested it on my lap. It took a few minutes to find a granola bar. At least I thought it was.

When I set down my bag, I grabbed that little flashlight.

I lit it and shone it on my lap to make sure it was my bar and bottle of water. It was.

Then before I shut it off, I wanted to see what was out there, beyond our table.

My view had been limited to that black wall of nothingness.

As soon as I aimed that flashlight outward, I jumped.

The woman with the blue shawl was in the same place I last saw her.

Crouched at the end of our table looking into our safety nook.

She was still in that crouching position, held up by the thick ash that came just above her waist. Enough to keep her propped up.

Her eyes were open, and she was covered in a layer of ash. Complete gray from head to toe with only two splashes of color. The hint of blue from her shawl and the red of blood as it created streaks in her skin. Like teardrops, the blood trickled down her face from the several places she had been impaled by shards of glass.

I kept that flashlight on her for a while. Staring.

Sometimes when you stare at something long enough it will change.

She did.

I gasped and jolted when I thought I saw her eyes blink. That was nothing compared to the scream of fright I released when she weakly croaked out, "Help me."

NINETEEN – ASHES TO ASHES

The plan to stay under the tables in the dark all night was over the moment everyone realized that woman was alive.

It was the only time since leaving the camp that I saw people come together.

The "every man for himself" mentality of the highway was out the window.

It made me feel better for humanity.

When Lorna asked for help, unable to move, still in shock, I screamed. Then my scream that was more from a jump scare turned into, "She's alive. Someone help! She's alive!"

And everyone crawled out.

A woman named Thea was the first one over.

She trudged through the ash, lifting each leg as if it weighed a ton, but rushing to Lorna.

A call for help. A call answered.

Flashlights everywhere turned on.

Even though we'd all need our flashlights in the hours and days ahead, everyone kept theirs lit. Those who survived in that diner found a way to create light, including a makeshift fire pit in a large soup cauldron.

That was after. After they helped Lorna.

That large fire pit did something else.

It illuminated the bodies.

A lot of people died.

Thea mention that most of them probably died from suffocation. That was a comment she made in between barking out orders.

"I need water," she called out. "Someone get me water. Can we move these bodies?"

"How did they all die?" I heard someone say.

"Probably suffocated," Thea answered as she worked.

That made sense. The ash wasn't like the stuff that remained after burning paper. It was thick, like stone. We didn't sink into it too much. The heavy ash kept Lorna in an upright position.

Thea was my mom's age, only she seemed tougher.

I saw the struggle as she tried to hurry through the ash. A couple men moved a table upright. Then two more came over and lifted Lorna.

Her legs were still bent, her hands rolled inward.

"She's in shock," Thea said. "Lay her down. Can anyone see if there's a first aid kit in the kitchen."

I started to crawl out, my bottle of water in hand.

"Stay here," Ben said.

"I'll be back. I want to see."

I knew Ben well. He would have come with me, but he was hurt. He just didn't want to admit it.

Leaving my backpack behind, I emerged from under that table. I had my small flashlight but didn't turn it on. So many were lit.

Thea was straightening Lorna's legs.

She then touched her neck and lowered her head to her chest.

"Come on, Lorna, hang on," Thea said.

I extended my bottle of water. "Here."

Thea looked at me. "Thank you. Thank you so much."

"Is she alive?" I asked.

"Yes. She is. She's in shock."

A man came over. "The first aid kit is on the wall. Some bandages, aspirin."

"Should be saline eyewash in there somewhere. Can you check?"

The man nodded.

She turned to me. "I have a bag, It's green; about the size of a gym bag. It's somewhere on the other side of the counter. Can you look?"

I nodded. "Yes."

"Thank you." Thea opened my water bottle and poured it slowly on Lorna's face.

I just watched for a second, then went to the counter.

It was a lunch counter, like they had in the movies. I passed the man who sought out the first aid kit as I went behind the counter. He was carrying items.

It was dark. Everything was black back there, and I turned on my little light. The beam wasn't wide; so, it took a lot of moving it around until I found it. It was in the corner near a bare spot without ash. Probably where Thea was sitting.

The bag was heavy and sturdy, more like a canvas case.

I carried it back out.

I heard her speaking to Lorna, calling her by name.

"I have it," I said, and noticed she had things sprawled out on the table next to Lorna. A bottle of saline, gauze, and other bandages.

"Oh, thank you. Could you open it. It zips and opens like a book, she said." Then she turned her head. "Can I please have a light?"

I wasn't sure how I was going to give her a light and open the case. So, I opted for opening the case first.

"Hold it open for me. Like a book. Can you?"

I nodded, and once I unzipped it, I opened it. "Is she your friend?" I asked. "You know her name?"

First Aid Kit Guy aimed his flashlight on the case.

"She was walking," Thea answered, grabbing items from the case. "I picked her up. We just met." She glanced at the First Aid Guy. "I'm gonna need your help. What's your name?"

"Don."

"Don, one hand on the light. I'll need you to hand me things. I'm gonna do this one first." She turned Lorna's head. "This one is going to bleed."

"I'm ready," Don said.

Thea pulled back the shawl. It snagged on a huge chuck of glass that protruded from the side of Lorna's head.

Holding what looked like large tweezers, Thea lowered her hand to the glass. "Light."

Don moved the light.

Thea pulled the shard of glass from Lorna's head.

Watching it come out went right through me, like a fork against a metal plate. I winced watching blood ooze out of the wound. Thea poured saline on it, then placed gauze over it. "Don, could you hold this? Give it pressure."

"Yeah, sure." Don reached down.

Thea looked at me. "Are you okay?"

"I'm fine. Are you a doctor?"

"I am." She moved on to the smaller pieces on Lorna's face.

"My brother is hurt. When you're done, can you help him?"

Thea glanced at me. "How did he get hurt?"

"Some man beat him up."

"How old is your brother?"

"Sixteen."

Thea gave me a gentle smile and nodded. "Absolutely. I will check on him."

"Thank you." I don't know why, but I really wanted to cry at that second. My lips quivered and started to pucker, but I held it in.

I was so happy at that moment. I crawled out from that booth. I was helping Thea, and she was going to help my brother.

<><><><>

It took Lorna's call for help for people to lose fear. In the black of it all, stuck in the thick ash, she probably thought she was alone.

Then I turned on the light.

When she cried out, I did.

People heard.

They crawled out from their hiding spaces.

I truly believed if Lorna hadn't cried out for help, then we'd all still be quiet and in the complete dark.

It was about the time someone had the idea for the caldron makeshift fire pit that Thea was able to check on Ben.

It took a lot of convincing to get Ben out from under the table.

It was a reminder to me that Ben was slightly different from everyone.

It was reminiscent of when he was little and would hide from loud noises. It was fourth grade all over. Hiding under the desk because a bully got to him.

Don't slide backwards, Ben.

When he was with me, my brother was open and talked to me. Around others, especially strangers, he recoiled, blinked a little more than usual, and withdrew.

Please come out, Ben. Please.

Eventually he crawled out and let Thea examine him.

"How, I don't know; but nothing is broken," she said. "The nose is badly bruised. It's not broke. You're a tough kid."

Ben half shrugged.

Thea cleaned him up and stopped him from crawling back under the table. "It's dirty under there. It's dirty everywhere, I know. But I want to keep an eye on you. Plus, you need to eat." She raised her voice. "Everyone needs to eat and have water."

Don spoke up. "There are cases of water in the back. They're covered in ash, but the water is fine."

"Good." Thea said. "Let's get them. Everyone needs some water. Let's see what else we can find in the kitchen."

Thea was a leader; I could tell that. The way she took command, she probably was an ER doctor. One of those that barked orders and got things done.

She got a few people to volunteer and move bodies to one side of the diner.

I volunteered.

Thea told me "No" at first, but I insisted. I didn't want to just sit around and do nothing.

She handed me a broom.

"Okay, I get what you want me to do," I said. "But this broom isn't going to make a difference."

"There are bodies under the ash. You wanted to help," she said. "Start moving the broom through the ash to find them."

I was still helping with the bodies, but in a different way. I was fishing for them so the others could pull them out.

Someone had estimated there were about twenty bodies in the ash. Those who were in the center of the room or didn't hide under anything.

Carefully, I moved the broom. An apocalypse archeologist, carefully removing layers.

I had located three, and then I gave up. The tiny hand poked from the gray ashes, and all I thought about was Ruby. I didn't want to see the child. I couldn't.

That poor little kid, boy or girl, I didn't know. As harsh as it sounded, I hoped her family was in the ash with her because it would be horrible for them.

Who was I kidding?

It was horrible for a lot of people.

Those behind us out west that didn't make it out, and those ahead of us out east that didn't have a clue what was coming.

I handed the broom to Thea and said I was sorry.

I knew Ruby would be heavily on my mind, especially after seeing her hand.

I went back to my comfort zone: My brother.

Someone made soup. It wasn't really hot, but it was good, and I didn't have to dig into my bag for my supplies.

I stayed in the booth next to my brother. It was getting colder and darker, and I grew more sad by the minute.

I just wanted to be home.

TWENTY – THE LONE RANGER

June 17 – Van Tassel, WY

There was no early morning sunlight. No night-to-day; only shades of dark.

Everyone was gathering what belongings they had.

"Remember," Don called out. "No one leaves alone. We leave together. We stick together. It's safer that way."

He walked over to me and Ben and handed us a small plastic bag. It was white with a yellow smiley face on it.

"He's some food for you two," Don said. "I tried to divide everything evenly. Stick close, okay?"

I nodded. "Thank you."

"Now as soon as we get Lorna situated, we'll head out."

I knew they had made a makeshift gurney for her using a broken table. "You guys are gonna carry her all the way to Nebraska?" I asked.

Don chuckled. "We're less than a half a mile to Nebraska. We're carrying her until we find help."

When he walked away, I looked at Ben. "We're almost in Nebraska."

"Who knew we'd walk from Wyoming to Nebraska," he joked.

We both laughed a little. It was good to see it. I think we both felt better after some sleep and knowing that we weren't going to be walking alone.

The people from the diner seemed nice.

Not including us, Ben said he counted fourteen.

Lorna was doing better. She was looking around, talking. I hoped she would get up and walk because I knew carrying her was going to be hard.

Like Don said, hopefully, they'd find help.

The Lorna carriers were the first ones out of the rubble. Then others followed.

It wasn't easy; I could see that. Climbing out a window or through what was left of the door. Fighting the weight of the ash.

I could hear them hollering back to "watch your step," and the ash was deceiving.

Comments such as:

"It's hard to walk out here."

"Why is it so cold?"

"Are we going the right way?"

Carried to us as we brought up the rear, nearly the last ones out.

Then I heard something else.

The "neigh" of a horse. It started a chain reaction of people calling out.

The horse. The trotting. I instantly got excited.

Pops.

It had to be Pops.

Riding in to save the day, just as I imagined. He'd take Lorna on the horse. Of course, he would.

They made that sound. A frustrated fluttering.

"Pops," I said to Ben. "I bet it's Pops."

"Marty, I don't think…"

"It has to be." I secured my facemask and moved to the window. I felt impatient waiting on Ben who moved at his own slow pace.

I wanted to see Pops. Run out and hug him, but I quickly realized that wasn't going to happen.

Not yet.

There was a horse. Actually, two. And they were harnessed to something I had seen a couple of days earlier.

A covered wagon.

The same one from the museum.

Driving it was Sam.

Sluggishly, against the grain of the ash, we made our way out just as Sam hopped from the driver's seat, and a couple of boys, including Clarence, came from the back.

They looked as bad as we did.

Sam talked to Don and the boys. They helped the Lorna carriers lift her into the covered wagon.

His mouth and nose were covered, and all I could see were Sam's eyes.

They shifted away from Don, and he saw us.

They widened as he hurried over to us.

"You guys are okay," he said with relief. "Well, sort of…" he looked at Ben. "What happened to you?"

Ben shook his head. "Nothing. It's fine."

"I thought for sure Clark found you," Sam said.

"He did," I replied. "We didn't go with him. We found out our grandfather left on horseback to search for us. We just didn't want to be in a truck and him not see us."

"Clark was a few miles ahead of us," Ben said.

"Good," Sam replied. "Then he made it to Nebraska. They said the cloud broke just past the border, right before the military set up."

"How do you know?" I asked.

"Radio. We had a signal for a second."

"Us, too."

Sam reached out and placed a hand on Ben's arm. "We're all together. I'm sorry I was so harsh on you. You did a good job taking care of your sister."

"She took care of me," Ben said.

I shook my head. "We took care of each other."

"And that's what we'll do right now," Sam said.

I was glad to be walking with others, but also happy I was

with my brother.

Having been so wrapped up in looking for Pops when I heard that horse, I didn't bother to look around.

We had emerged into another world. One void of color and warmth. Cars buried in two-feet-thick, mud-looking ash, as more fell from the sky.

Steady.

Slow.

Accumulating.

The horse-drawn wagon had to make its way on the side of the road. Makeshift masks covered the horses' mouths; but I didn't think it would do any good, and I worried about the horses.

If we could not breathe it in, how could they?

Those of us walking stopped for breaks, and Sam continued on, trying to get Lorna some help.

It never was light. It reminded me of a rainy evening before the rain arrived.

But it was on our second stop that I saw it on my pants.

Blood.

My mind went to Jean Jacket Man and what I had done. A sickening lump hit my stomach. It seemed like a dream, and I wanted it to be. But it wasn't.

I took his life. Even thought he was hurting my brother, I still took a life, and that was something I would have to live with. A guilt I would carry.

Ben hadn't mentioned it again, and I wanted to talk about it.

It wasn't the right time.

Maybe when we got home.

I was scared, too. Would I get in trouble? Would someone find out? Or were laws tossed out the window? I hoped not; because if they were, we were all in trouble.

We walked a lot in silence, Ben and I; not because there was nothing to say, but because we didn't want to inhale too much ash. People coughed; not too bad, but I guessed it would worsen. Plus, it gave me a chance to listen to what they said.

Some people had actually watched the news and learned all they could.

One man sounded really knowledgeable as he walked and talked with a woman. "They say global temperatures will drop ten degrees."

"That doesn't sound too bad."

"Not too bad?" the guy scoffed. "We're talking most of North American being on big chunk of ice."

Was he right? Would the eruption send us into an ice age?

I looked up at the sky. It was so gray and dark. It was June, and it was colder than any temperature I had ever known. Of course, I was from Los Angeles. It did get cold in December; but it felt so much colder walking that road.

There were some bright spots in the journey.

Seeing the Nebraska sign.

Stopping at the Wendy's and getting crackers.

And the bright spotlights that danced in the distance on the horizon.

They were blurry, shining through the dust cloud of ash, but they were bright. And the closer we walked, the more I could hear shouting, some motor sound, and the beeping of someone going in reverse.

Life.

Not that I didn't think there was life out there. I knew everyone was going east.

To me, we hit a milestone.

It had been a while since I had seen the wagon. Sam had gotten Lorna inside with help from several of the boys from camp.

I wondered if Clark was there. Surely, he passed through. Did he run into Pops? Would he know he was our grandfather?

Approaching the spotlights, the taillights of the trucks were visible, along with a small strobe light on top of the canvas coverings on one of the vehicles.

A makeshift fence made of those long, bright plastic barriers. It didn't block completely, there was an opening, and flares lined up to mark the road.

"Pedestrians to the right please," someone shouted. "Pedestrians to the right. Clear the way for vehicles."

We moved to the right with everyone else. It was like a dream. Cars, trucks, and people walking, kicking up the ash, creating a foggy cloud.

We'd see people vanish the farther from us they got.

I didn't know what was next. Did we keep going? Were we to stop? It wouldn't take long before I found out.

They had a camp set up with lots of tents and sounds of confusion.

I stayed close to Ben.

<><><><>

Two people, a man and a woman, had on jackets with a patch that said "FEMA".

They directed people on foot.

A line had formed, not a long one. But it moved slowly.

They were frustrated, and their patience was tried. I could tell by the way they talked and directed people. Saying they didn't have answers to give, to move forward, they would be evacuating in groups.

"I'm a doctor," Thea told the woman. "Not sure if you need any."

"Actually, we do. If you go to that tent," she pointed to the right. "Just check in, and they'll tell you where we need you."

"Why are we checking in?" Thea asked.

"We're trying to get everyone's names. Cross-check people that are searching. If you can just check in. Thank you."

Thea stepped forward, and we followed her.

"No. You two in that tent." She indicated to the left.

"Why are they going to a different tent?" questioned Thea.

"Are either of them eighteen?"

Both Ben and I shook our heads.

"We're making sure all the children are safe; so we can try to connect them with family."

Thea nodded and looked at me. "That's good. Sam will probably be right in for you. I'm sure the other kids from the camp are there."

"Okay," I muttered, kind of nervous that Thea was going in a totally different direction.

We went in the kids tent; the apocalypse version of the kids' table.

Inside, were the boys from camp and about six others. No one was really young. No babies or little kids.

The woman in there seemed kind. She took our names and gave us a pack. In it, was food, water, and even candy.

It was nice to not be in so much ash. To see faces without masks. To have some sort of explanation. The woman was gentle and much more patient than the two outside of the tent.

Everyone asked the same question.

What happened? What would happen?

She explained that Yellowstone erupted, and it wasn't done. That experts expected the remaining eruption to occur in the next several days.

"You're safe," she said. "The big portion already erupted. We are expecting more ash. We just need to get out before it gets so deep that it clogs engines."

"What are you doing with us?" I asked.

"We're finding out where everyone lives and trying to get word to families." She shrugged. "We have some time, and this is a safe place. No one is going to hurt you here." She looked at Ben, apparently noticing his bruises. "We'll get you in a tent where you can relax. This is just a check-in area." The woman then looked behind us. "Can I help you?"

Sam stood in the doorway of the tent. "Sorry. Yeah. I'm here to collect my kids."

"Oh," she replied. "Which ones are yours?"

"That one, that one…" Sam pointed to us. "That one and that one."

"You look way too young…"

"Oh, no; they aren't *my* kid kids. They were in my care at

camp, and I want to get them back home. A friend, Clark..." he smiled at us. "He got a minibus for me to take."

"Clark's here?" I asked brightly.

Sam nodded. "Yeah. He was actually waiting here for you guys. He was worried. He's a good guy."

The woman made this squeamish face. "I'm sorry. Unless you're a blood relative, I can't let you take these kids. We're going to try to reach their parents."

"I can take them to their parents," Sam argued.

"I'm sorry."

"This is ridiculous. They want to go with me."

"I know they do," she said. "And I feel bad, but we really..." she huffed, showing for the first time some irritation. "Sir, can you please..." she spoke to someone else. "Step outside. There should be no one in here unless they are family."

"Well," he said. "I'm pretty sure as shit those two belong to me."

My eyes widened. My heart skipped a beat, and with a gasp, I spun around. "Pops!"

I ran to him as fast as I could, narrowly beating Ben to wrap our arms around him. I have never seen my brother so happy and excited. I had never seen him hug anyone like he hugged Pops.

Pops' arms were big enough to wrap around us both.

He came for us. He had found us.

I always knew he was a big guy. But at that moment, to me, Pops was larger than life.

TWENTY-ONE – STEADY FOR A MOMENT

In the years I have known Pops, and that was most of my life, I had never seen him wear anything other than jeans or the overalls he loved so much. To see him wearing camouflage pants and an Army sweatshirt was just odd. He looked so serious and strong. I pictured in my mind: Pops snuck into camp and pretended he was a general or something.

The nice lady in the check-in tent for kids asked Pops a few questions; but there really wasn't any doubt we were a family. Not the way we held onto him.

Sam was stunned.

"I'll have to tell Clark," Sam said with a shake of his head. "He was waiting for your grandkids."

"Clark?" Pops asked. "You mean that guy that looks like Crocodile Dundee?"

I laughed. "I thought the same thing."

"That's the one," Sam replied. "You met him, I take it?"

"Yeah. And we both were waiting on these two. And I didn't put two and two together. Neither of us did. Maybe he did. I don't know. I was just worried." Pops shrugged.

Ben smiled. He just watched Pops with wonder. Just like I did.

He was so strong.

I felt so safe with him.

They assigned us a tent for the night. The next bus going east would leave after breakfast and we'd be home, back on the ranch.

There was a lot of traffic moving through, we could have gotten a ride possibly. But Thea told Pops that we'd been out there, and she just wanted to make sure we were fine before we left.

He understood. He'd watched a lot of people get sick from the ash.

I had hoped the other kids from camp would be on the bus; but they had to wait for family or else they'd go to a special shelter in four days.

Ben and I were lucky.

There was one older man in the tent, and he had the corner cot. He was sleeping on his side, his back toward us when we walked in.

He wasn't as old as Pops, but he seemed it. He coughed a lot and had a little oxygen tank next to him.

He said his name was Mr. Billings, and we didn't need to be quiet. He was a heavy sleeper, and noise never bothered him.

We collected our supper in the tent that had food. A roll and bowl of stew, taking it back to the tent.

Before we did all that, we were told to shower and get all the ash off. They had special tents for that. They gave us clean clothes in a bag, ash free.

Our new clothes were Army PT gray sweats and sweatshirt. The word "Army" printed in black. They were soft and warm. The tents were cold; but with the sweatsuits, blankets, and warm stew, I wasn't that cold.

There was a heating can in the middle of the tent; but it wasn't lit.

"It's not that bad," Pops told us. "Eat up."

Ben asked him. "When did you get here?"

"Right when they closed the road. I couldn't get through. Even on foot. I'm an original here," Pops said. "I gave you the route, and they told me if I just wait, you'd come through here if you took Twenty."

"We did," I said. "We took your route."

"Told you that Red-Edit was right, and it was all you, Marty, that had me searching."

"What happened to the horse?" I asked. "Is it here?"

Pops shook his head. "I had to leave him at Stan's Feed and Field. He has him in the barn. He's supposed to get ahold of George to come and get him. Not sure if he did."

"He didn't," I told him. "We got a text from George saying you were on your way. I can't believe you walked."

"I walked a lot farther in my day," Pops replied. "Just have to pace yourself. Got a lot of information while I was here. New clothes, too." He smiled. "Also, some useful information. We can talk about that later.

I paused in eating and shivered, hunching my shoulders. "Aren't you cold?"

"No. I'm used to the cold and snow. It will only get worse," said Pops. "They're talking a mini ice age. Snowball earth. One of the things I learned here."

"Will every place freeze over?" I asked.

"No, not every place." Pops shook his head and dipped his bread in the gravy. "The farther south, the better it will be."

"How is that possible?"

Ben answered. "Marty, come on. Do you know how big Yellowstone was? It blew enough dirt and ash into the sky to block the sun enough to make it cold."

"What about the farm?" I asked.

"Ranch," Pops corrected. "Nope. It will freeze over."

That made me gasp. "Pops. The animals."

"You mean my horses and cattle?" he questioned. "The beauty of it is those are a commodity. While waiting on you kids, I was able to get on the commodity conservation. It's where they give you a piece of land for your livestock. And well, I don't suppose it will be as big as my land. But it's something."

Ben looked at Pops with a smile. "Come on. For real? Commodity conservation. Is that a Pops tale to make us not worry, or a real thing?"

From across the room, coughing Mr. Billings grumbled out.

"It's real. A lot of ranchers passed through. And farmers. He just didn't show up with his livestock. Just his mouth."

"Yep," Pops nodded. "But I set it up. Main transport leaves Teetersville on July third."

"Second," Billings corrected. "I paid attention."

"You're right. The second. I got the information in my bag," Pops said. "We move everything to Teetersville and wait to go. It'll be good for us to go south."

"How?" Ben asked. "You have to get the cattle and horses to Teetersville. Wherever that is."

"A hundred miles south of home," Pops said. "Bud Wheeler's next ranch over has a bull rack. We'll get that off of him. He sold everything else two years ago. He's been sitting on that bull rack for his retirement fund. I don't think he'll mind parting with it during the ice age. I'll write him a check for a million dollars."

"Do you have a million?" I asked.

Pops shook his head. "Nope. But I think it'll be a long time before he finds a bank to cash it."

That made me laugh. I was so happy to be with Pops. I felt better for Ben as well. We were in good hands; and after a good night's sleep, we'd be on our way home.

To me, the dark of things was behind us.

TWENTY-TWO – NOT SO FAST

June 18 – Chadron, NE

Seeing Clark seated in the front of the bus was surprising. Apparently, his engine stopped running because of the ash.

Clogged or something.

It left me wondering if that would happen to the bus we were on.

I told Ben, and he said the bus was bigger, higher off the ground, and the ash wasn't as thick as it was before the camp.

More than likely, it was just an old crappy truck that broke down and Clark didn't want to admit it.

Not that I was picking on Clark. I liked him.

Sometimes, a part of me blamed Clark for Ben getting beat up. Had we just let Jean Jacket Man rob us, we would have been at the diner anyhow and safely in the camp the next day.

Jean Jacket Man.

Sigh.

Every time he came to my mind, I felt a thump in my belly. A feeling I knew would never go away.

It would haunt me for the rest of my life.

I wanted to talk about it. Then again, I didn't. I was ashamed and guilty. I wasn't sure if there was a judging afterlife. But surely if there was a hell, I was burning in it.

I said goodbye to Thea. She was staying back at the camp until it moved south in two weeks. She said she was probably going to the camp on the Texas/Mexico border. Maybe I would one day see her.

As for me and Ben, we were going to be back with our mom, George, and Ruby.

According to Pops, our new home was going to be in Austin. At least we wouldn't be living in a tent city like so many other people.

"Pops might be wrong," Ben whispered to me before we got on the bus.

"What do you mean?"

"Just be prepared if he's not right about moving to Austin, okay?"

"Why would he be wrong?"

"Come on, Marty."

"Ben," I said. "When people slip or have dementia, do they stay in that delusion constantly?"

"I don't know." He shrugged. "Just be ready for no moving cows and horses. Just us leaving."

I hated he thought that way, but that was another thing about my brother. He took a lot of things literal and had a built-in cynic factor.

His words stayed with me. But I believed Pops. I really did.

<><><><>

The ash continued to fall. And when we were leaving, they were predicting another eruption. The last, which they predicted would happen in two days. Wherever we were, we were safe from that rolling power ash cloud. It wasn't supposed to be that big, but enough to add the final straw in darkening the skies.

Someone said about an inch of ash covered the roads. It was hard to tell. In fact, it was hard to tell what anything looked like.

It was so gray, and the tires on the ash-covered road just created a shroud of dust out the windows. I didn't know how the bus driver could see.

He was a soldier; and he didn't seem bothered by it. We didn't drive fast. I understood why.

We sat two rows behind him. Pops on one side of the bus, me and Ben in a seat on the other. Clark sat in front of us. I didn't really look back, but I knew the bus was full.

"Are you sure you guys want off in Chadron?" the driver asked. "I heard you mention something about Teetersville. I'm mean, I'm headed to Kearny before Kansas. I can drop you there."

"That's very nice of you, son," Pops answered. "The reason we're going to Teetersville is to meet up with that government livestock transport. And no reason to go there without my livestock."

"That's true, sir. Are you sure they weren't transported already?"

"Positive. My son probably already got the bull rack from the neighboring ranch. We'll take that."

I listened to Pops talk, thinking about what Ben had said. Pops sounded so sure. He had to be right.

"Why is this bus going to Kansas?" I asked. "Is it safe there?"

"Right now, yes," the driver replied. "In another couple weeks, it won't be. It's where they are moving people out of. It's a huge exodus."

"To where?" I questioned.

"Lots of places. All south. Wherever they go, I guess. Texas, Florida, Mexico... even some cruise ships are being stocked for the long term."

"So how do they determine where people go? Alphabetical? Skills?"

Clark turned around and looked at me. "That's a good question."

"There is no rhyme or reason for the general population that is evacuating," the driver answered. "Just put people where they can survive. I'm sure skills play a big factor. But for the most part, it's just an exodus."

"So, people don't know where they're going?" I questioned.

"No. Maybe when they leave Kansas, but there's not really a

say-so," the drive replied. "If they're using government evacuation measures, they have nowhere to go. So, as long as they survive. Right?"

I glanced at Clark. "What about you?"

"I'm a nomad," Clark said. "My home's gone. Heck, I'll play the survivor lottery. Maybe I'll end up in Florida or on one of those cruises."

"If you find out," the driver said. "That your livestock went ahead, another bus will be through here in three days. Same time. You can catch it."

Then Ben quietly spoke, "Did something happen in Chadron? I mean, you seem surprised we're getting off."

"Well, yeah. They started a mass evacuation a couple days ago," the driver answered. "I mean, a sweep of the state. Nebraska is in a danger zone and is one of the states they did mandatory evacuations. Just might be empty."

I turned my head to Pops. He had this closed-mouthed, assured look to him. He shook his head and reached over. "Your mom and George are there. We go as a family. Don't worry."

For a split second, I heard Ben's words in my head. And for that split second, I doubted Pops. I quickly dismissed it. Whether or not he had gotten things right or was mistaken, the fact remained, Pops trekked on foot during a super volcano eruption to find us.

I would never doubt him again.

No matter what. Even if he were wrong, I'd find a way to make it right.

TWENTY-THREE – GONE

We passed through town, driving straight down the main street. Not that Chadron was ever bustling, but it was particularly quiet and empty. The few cars that remained on the road were covered in a layer of ash. There were no tire tracks on the street. And despite that it was daylight, it was still hazy and dark. Every store looked dark, no light… no life.

In the last few miles before Chadron, Clark had decided he was going to join us. Then suddenly, as the bus came to a stop, he changed his mind.

It was weird.

Especially because he asked me my mother's name and did I have a picture of her.

I pulled out my phone. I was able to charge it at the camp, not that it mattered, there wasn't a signal.

I showed him and he thanked me.

There was something about Clark that didn't feel right. Not that he was bad, but from the moment he saved us from Jean Jacket Man, I always felt he was supposed to be with us.

Like, why were we told about him if he was only popping in and out of the survival picture?

Maybe fate had a bigger role for him in our lives.

It sure didn't feel like it when we stepped off that bus and watched him wave as the bus moved on.

In what seemed ironic, the bus left us off at the parking lot of the super Walmart.

A frequent topic of conversation, the once bustling establishment was eerily bare and empty.

Once the bus had gone from sight, it left a cloud of dust and a dismal silence.

We stood on the main road, at the edge of an empty ash covered parking lot with the dark super center behind us.

"How far are we?" Ben asked.

"About four miles," Pops answered. "Bud Wheeler's place is closer. It's a little bit of a walk, but hey, we all walked more recently, haven't we?"

I nodded. "We have. I guess we should start, huh?"

Pops looked down at his watch. "Not so fast, it's early." He looked over his shoulder behind him. "Let's go shopping first."

Shopping?

Maybe Pops had a sudden urge to gather more supplies. Thinking about it, that wasn't a bad idea.

We walked across the parking lot toward the store.

As I expected, the doors were closed and locked.

Pops peeked in the front window. "Lucky for us, the power didn't go off long ago."

"How is that lucky?" I asked.

"Emergency lights are on," Pops said. "They only last about twelve hours. Now we can see."

"We need to get in there," Ben said.

"Ha. Step back." Pops walked toward the door, lifted the garbage can, and hurled it into the doors.

Garbage flew out everywhere as the can crashed through the window.

We stepped inside, and Pops grabbed a cart.

I expected the store to be empty and looted. After all, every movie I had seen showed people rushing to the store and grabbing products off shelves.

But the Walmart looked untouched. Like it just locked up, and no one bothered to go there.

It was strangely quiet, almost muffled. The ash seemed to do that to everything.

"What are we getting?" Ben asked. "Are we just gonna throw stuff in the cart?"

"No, no." Pops shook his head. "We have to be strategic. Food we can carry. Batteries. Lots of batteries. Flashlights. We'll hit the camping section. I'd say let's find warm clothes, but that will be impossible right now."

He was right. It was summer, and the only clothes would be lightweight.

"We just need to think survival and trade," Pops said. "But I have my thoughts. So just follow along and help me out."

"Pops?" I asked. "Don't you have a lot of stuff at your house?"

"I do. But… you never know." He pushed the cart forward. "You never know."

<><><><>

We were in the store for about an hour, and Pops methodically walked the aisles. He sent me over to the checkout lanes to grab more bags. I didn't understand why. We bagged everything that could fit in the bags. The rest was stacked in the overcrowded buggy.

Not much was said as we shopped. We followed him around and eventually out of the store.

Pops pushed the cart.

Ben offered; but it wasn't an easy task, and Pops claimed the task.

It was sluggish as we moved through the ash-layered parking lot and down the empty road.

Pops knew exactly what he was doing and where he was going.

We had walked about three blocks, and Pops turned the cart into the parking lot of Eb's Auto Care.

After peeking in the window, Pops broke it. Only this time, he asked if I would climb through for him.

It was a small window, and I was careful as I did it.

It smelled weird in there, like oil and mold. I unlocked the door for Pops. He walked straight through and to the back.

"Eb had a reputation of changing brakes when they didn't need changed," Pops said from the back room. "Never understood why people didn't learn to change their own brakes. It's not hard. Bingo."

I turned Ben, listening to Pops talk about Eb.

"The brake master." Pops emerged from the back and dangled a set of keys. "In the queue."

"What does that mean?" I asked.

"It means it was waiting." He walked to the door and pressed the button on the key fob. With a blip-blip, the taillights of a black sedan blinked. "We have a ride."

"What if the brakes are really bad?" I asked.

"We only have to go a mile. We'll be fine. We just need to get to Wheeler's place."

We had left the buggy outside the auto shop. And by the time we had returned, not even a few minutes later, ash had already covered the bags.

We pushed the cart to the black car and loaded everything inside. It was a squeeze even for me in the back seat to fit with all the stuff.

Pops got in and started the car. "Once we get to Wheeler's, just take the car, and I'll drive the rack."

"Who?" I asked.

"Ben."

"Me?" Ben asked. "I don't have a license."

"You're sixteen," Pops said.

"Doesn't mean I can drive. I don't know how to drive."

Pops reached for the door. "Why don't we try now."

"No." Ben shook his head. "No. I... I don't want to. I can't see. There's a lot of ash. I ..."

"I will," I cut in the conversation. "I'll drive."

Pops looked at me in the rearview mirror. "Alright. Ben, hop in the back."

"Seriously? You're gonna let her drive? That can *not* be safe."

"Someone has to drive. We're not unloading, loading, and

unloading these bags again. Hop in the back."

Ben groaned loudly as he opened the door. I smiled at him as I got out.

"Don't wreck," Ben told me.

"You're fine. The Walmart bags and toilet paper will cushion you."

I was excited. I walked around, and got in the driver's seat, even pulling it closer so my feet hit the pedals.

"Look at you, being a pro," Pops said as he got in.

"I watch my mom and asked a million questions about driving. Plus, I played that game at the pizza shop that acts like a race car."

"Right pedal gas Left brake," Pops explained. "This is the gear shift. We're going forward, so you need to only put it in drive."

"D."

"Yep."

I put my hand on the gear shift between the front seats and tried to move it. "It's stuck."

"Keep your foot on the brake, and push the button on the side with your thumb, and then move it," explained Pops.

"Oh my God," Ben commented from the back seat.

I did as instructed, and before Pops could tell me "easy", I touched the gas, and we flew forward.

Good thing I was fast and hit the brake, jerking us all back.

"Oh my God! Please, stop!" Ben yelled.

I laughed. "It has a kick."

Pops shook his head. "No, it doesn't. You're heavy-footed. Easy. Just tap it until you feel comfortable with it moving."

It took a few seconds of moving until I felt in control. After that initial go and hard stop, I didn't drive like newbies in a movie. I did good. Of course, Pops had to tell me to slow down.

It only took a few minutes to get to Mr. Wheeler's ranch.

As soon as we turned onto his long driveway, I could see his giant truck parked on the side of the barn.

"Is that it?" I asked.

"That's it," Pops replied.

"It doesn't look sturdy," I said.

"Well, yeah. Probably not. The newer trucks are metal now. It's old. But it will get the job done."

Ben asked from the back, "How many cows does it hold?"

"It's fifty-two thousand pounds. I can get my load in there. I sold a lot of heads last year. So, I only have thirty and a dozen horses. Used to have so many more. Just pull on up."

"I don't see Mr. Wheeler," I said.

"Looks like he evacuated." Pops leaned close to the windshield. "I don't see his Chevy. If he was here, he would have come out."

I pulled up to the barn, and Pops instructed for me to put the car in "park", I did.

He opened the door. "Keys will be in the barn. I'll be back."

I sat in the driver's seat, watching Pops go into the barn. He had to really pull the door to get it open, but he was inside a few minutes. Not too long, but close enough that I started to worry.

Then, he finally emerged with a big smile and dangled the keys.

"I'll be back," I told Ben and opened the door. "You got them?" I asked Pops.

"I do. Get back in the car."

"I want to make sure it starts for you."

Pops nodded and walked to the truck. It was huge and long. The front part was rusted a bit with some dents. The back end had high wooden slats that formed a box.

He opened the door and climbed up. It seemed a stretch for him. I didn't know how someone like George would be able to get in there.

I listened as the truck started, and then I heard Pops swear, "Son of a bitch."

"What's wrong?"

Leaving the truck running, Pops stepped out and pointed. "Get back to the car."

"What's wrong."

"Get in," he said as he walked to me. Once I was inside, he

leaned to the window. "Do you know how to get home?"

"Not really. Can I follow you?"

Pops shook his head. "I'll be kicking up way too much ash for you to see. No. You'll have to lead."

"I heard you swear. What…"

"We'll talk at home." Then Pops proceeded to give me what sounded like easy directions before walking back to the big truck.

"Ben, you can get up front."

"No, I'll stay safe in the back with the toilet paper."

I laughed. Maybe if there were other cars on the road, I would have been nervous to drive, but I wasn't. It was fun, and I was excited because we would be home soon.

The drive was easy, and Pops beeped just before the turns, so I didn't mess up.

Chadron was still foreign to me. Even though we visited it before, I didn't remember any directions.

I knew when we pulled up to the house, something wasn't right.

Pops' truck was out front, but George's car was not.

Suddenly, I felt like it was hard to breathe. A wave of anxiety swept over me when I saw a huge red X painted on the house next to the front door.

"Ben?" I peeped out.

The sound of the truck airbrakes rang out.

"Maybe they went looking for us," Ben suggested.

"Why would they do that? And what is that X?"

"I don't know."

I looked in the mirror when I heard the truck door behind us then back to the door. At the top of the X was the date of June seventeenth, on the left was E3, a zero to the right, and a zero at the bottom.

I jumped at the knock on my window. I wound it down.

"Shut it off. Let's go inside," Pops said.

"Pops, what's going on?" I asked.

"What is that X?" Ben questioned.

"That…" Pops pointed. "Is a FEMA marking. The top is the date it happened. The E3 means three evacuated. The zeros mean no dead or hazards."

I shook my head. "I don't understand."

"Looks like it happened yesterday," Pops replied. "George, Tess, Ruby… they're evacuated. They're gone."

TWENTY-FOUR – MILK SHAKE

Ben and Marty,
Hopefully, you won't see this because you'll both be safe in my arms. That you took an evacuation bus and ended up with us. We had to go. We had no choice. We either left with the evacuation caravan or they forced us on the bus. The danger for the area is high. Because despite what they are saying, the second eruption could be worse. If you get this, if you see this, please do not stay in Chadron. The keys to Pops' truck are in the kitchen. Find a way to get out. They say we are headed to Kansas City. After that, I don't know. George herded the livestock into the big barn for protection. They said someone would come for them. I hope they do. Be safe. We love you both very much.
Mom

All three of us had a different reaction to seeing that note left just inside the screen porch door.

I kept thinking, *They left us. They just left us?* And it bothered me that there wasn't even a note for Pops. Like they didn't believe he would find us. I felt heartbroken. Why and how could my mother just leave?

Ben seemed indifferent. Almost as if he wasn't surprised at all. As if he were ready to say, "Okay, what can happen next?"

Pops walked out. He just read the note, turned, and walked out the door.

"Ben, how?" I asked. "How could Mom just leave? Didn't she care? She just left us."

"It sounds like they didn't have a choice," Ben said calmly. "And Marty, it's not just us, you know. There is a chance it's really gonna get bad here. Mom had to worry about Ruby. She's just a baby. I'm glad she got her out of here. We'll be just fine. We're old enough to take care of ourselves. Ruby's not. We'll be fine. We have Pops."

Pops.

I looked left to right and remembered that he had walked out.

Stepping out of the house, I followed his footsteps in the ash. They led around the house, across the field to the big barn.

As I walked to him, I could see him just standing there, staring in the barn.

Pops looked stunned and shocked.

At first, I thought they were all gone. Then, as I got closer, I heard the livestock.

"Pops?" I said his name with question.

"I think... think the message they got about someone moving them was about me. They just didn't know it."

"They're all still here?" I asked.

"They're all still here. And if they're gonna be saved," Pops said. "I'm the one that has to do it."

<><><><>

There was some cornbread left in the tin container. It was stale, but it went well with the canned chili Pops made for supper.

We ate dinner in the dining room, lit by candles and some of the lanterns we got from Walmart.

"The way I see it," Pops said. "I'll need your help loading the pot tomorrow."

"Loading the pot?" I asked.

"Getting them on the truck," Pops explained. "I'd like for you to head to Kansas City after that. Take the car. It's already packed. But if you don't want to, you can wait for the bus. Although we don't know what's gonna happen with the next eruption."

"If we take the bus," Ben said. "Why don't you take the supplies?"

"Because they'll go to waste," Pops replied. "Truth be told, there's only a half a tank of gas in that truck. It'll get me three quarters of the way to Teetersville, and I won't be able to lug all those supplies."

"If the truck is only getting you near Teetersville," I asked. "How are you gonna get the rest of the way there with the cattle and horses?"

"Old fashioned way," Pops said. "I'll do a drive. Take them from the truck and drive them down."

That didn't make any sense to me. Drive them? Pops must have seen the confusion on my face.

"It means, I'll herd them and lead them by horse," Pops explained.

"Alone?" Ben asked. "Can you do that alone? No, wait. You can't."

"I have to try. I'll probably lose about thirty percent, but I am saving seventy." Pops stood. "I'm gonna get another cup of coffee."

I watched Ben more than Pops. He kept a stare on Pops when he left the room. Then Ben looked at me.

"Marty, I can't let him do this alone."

"He's not gonna let you help."

"Then I won't give him a choice. I just can't let him. I saw movies, Marty. He's not gonna be able to gather them and keep them together if he's alone."

"Ben, we don't know where Mom is going. If you stay with Pops, you'll lose track of them."

"Then I'll look for them or they'll find me," Ben replied. "If they're sending Ranchers to certain places, Mom will find me."

"What happened to you not being sure if Pops was right or if he was really was given a piece of land? You said it might not be true."

"It might not be," Ben said. "Ain't that all the more reason to go with Pops?"

"Take the journey with him no matter where it leads?"

Ben nodded. "As long as he isn't alone."

I exhaled heavily. "You're right. He came for us. We shouldn't leave him. You know he's gonna argue with…"

No warning.

No slow build vibration that let us know it was coming,

In the middle of our conversation, cutting me off mid-sentence, was a boom.

An explosion that sounded in the distance. Immediately, the house shook violently. At the same time, a rumbling noise filled the air.

The windows rattled and I felt like I was in a shaker.

It lasted thirty seconds, but it seemed longer.

Just enough time to dive under the table, but then it was over.

The "thump-thump-thump" of Pops' running footsteps caused me to rush from under the table. I heard him run out the door and to the porch, and I followed. Ben ran with me.

Pops stood twenty feet from the house, just staring out.

I joined him as he stared at the sky.

There was no fireball. No looking like the sky was ablaze. It was slightly brightened; as if there were an extra bright full moon.

Nothing spectacular.

It wasn't quiet though. The cows and horses were loud. The sounds of their confusion and anxiety carried to us.

"Was that it, Pops?" I asked. "Do you think that was it?"

"Yeah. Yeah. I think so." Pops placed his hands on his hips. He stared outward. A soundtrack of animal noises added to the tension. "I'm thinking tomorrow we better all head out early. Real early. I think…" he said. "I think we may be out of time."

TWENTY-FIVE – BAD FEELING

June 19

For the first hour after the explosion, or whatever it was, I hid.

Remembering the diner, I cleared out the pots and pans from the lower cabinet in the kitchen and hid there.

I didn't want to be near any windows when that ash cloud blasted through.

It never came.

Not, at least, in the way I expected.

Pops and Ben left the house and were doing something outside while I hid. They didn't ask me to help, and I didn't bother offering.

I was gun shy over that ash cloud.

In that cabinet with my lantern, along with the two fluffy pillows from the couch, I sat in silence. Alone.

I don't know how long I sat there, but the cabinets opened, and Pops was there.

"I don't know how you fit in here," he said. "I don't know how I'm crouching like this. I'm definitely gonna need help up."

"Is it over?" I asked.

"Not by a long shot. But Ben said you probably were scared of the pyroclastic cloud."

I nodded.

"It didn't come. A lot of things could have caused it to miss us. Not sure what they are. I'm a rancher, not a volcano guy. Your brother told me in no uncertain terms you two are coming with me."

"We are. We can't leave you, Pops."

"You realize, your mom may not find us for a while."

"I figure if they ask where they put the ranchers," I said. "They'll find us."

Pops nodded. "They don't think I made it to you."

"You don't know that."

"Was my name on that note?" he asked.

"No."

"Yeah. Well, anyhow… I want you guys to drive to Kansas. There's no time to wait for that bus. But if you are insistent on doing this with me… well, you'll have to be trained."

"Okay, I'll train."

"The Pops speed training."

I nodded.

"Come on out. We'll start."

"Okay."

Pops moved and grimaced. "Damn it. My knees are locked up." He slammed his hand on the counter above me and used that for leverage. I could hear his knees creak as he stood and grunted.

I grabbed onto Pops' hand and crawled out.

"You're gonna have to be braver than this, Marty."

"I've been brave."

"I know. But you have to keep being that way," he said. "No more hiding. You have to be tough. It's a hard world now and gonna be harder. If something scares you… well, you just face it, chest out and say, 'I got this'. I need you to promise me you're going to be brave."

I stood up straight. "I promise, Pops."

"Good, now let's go do Pops' speed cattle-drive training."

I nodded. I didn't know what it all meant or what I would be doing for his speed training, but I was ready.

We never left the house. In fact, we didn't even leave the living room.

Pops had just about two hours battery on the battery backup to his laptop, and he popped in an old movie; and we huddled around the screen to watch.

I thought it was a training film. Instead, it was a western with an actor who reminded me of Pops. A big, towering guy named John Wayne. Pops wasn't as rough around the edges as the actor was. But he was every bit as strong. The movie was about a rancher who hired a bunch of boys to move his cattle four hundred miles.

Pops said we would have to move his livestock nearly as far, and we had the road to our advantage.

The battery died before the movie ended. In fact, it died when the bad men were scaring one of the boys.

It made me think of how long ago that movie was made and how people really weren't any different in the wild west than they were in a world falling apart now.

"They got the cattle to where they needed to be," Pops said. "That's all you need to know about the end."

I knew it wasn't going to be easy. Even though there were only three of us, we had a lot less cattle than the movie.

Pops would tell us what to do.

I learned we just needed to keep them moving and keep them together. And whatever I did, Pops said not to trust the cattle.

They were big, moved on emotion, startled easy, and could do a lot of damage.

It sounded easier said than done, and it didn't look easy in that movie either.

I don't know why I had a bad feeling. Pops was a professional. He'd been doing the ranch stuff his entire life.

That wasn't it.

It was the morning. My bad feeling confirmed when I woke a few hours later to the sound of a loud "crack".

A foot of ash had fallen. It was heavy and caved in the back porch roof.

It had a dead silence to it all, and I was alone in the house.

My search for Ben and Pops brought me to the back window where I saw them loading the last few horses in the truck.

Both of them wore red ponchos. Ben's looked brand new, and I wondered if Pops had a stash.

I didn't get a poncho. Pops had a red raincoat for me. Just as bright red as the ponchos.

"Red will stand out in this ash," Pops said. "We'll need that."

With the truck called a "bull rack" packed and ready, Pops took a quiet moment to say goodbye to the only home he had ever known.

He looked a little sad. The weight of the move was heavier on him than the ash on the house.

It was time to go. The plan to take the second vehicle was out the window. It wouldn't make it in the ash.

There was enough fuel to get close; if the truck didn't choke out before that.

All three of us loaded in, like the cattle and horses, then slowly pulled away.

TWENTY-SIX – MILE MARKER SEVENTEEN

Our journey took us on roads that traced the edge of the mountains. None of them were a straight, flat shot. Which made things scary with the falling ash and accumulation.

Pops kept a steady pace. If we drove at the speed limit, under normal conditions, we would be close.

We couldn't do that.

When we neared Alliance, Nebraska; there were a lot of trees. And it helped shield the road from the ash; but the branches bent downward from the weight. Some brushed against the top of the truck as we drove through them.

It was a long shot, Pops said. But one we had to take.

The fuel gauge dipped near empty. And as we pulled into the empty town, Pops turned the truck into an EP gas station.

He didn't shut off the ignition because he didn't want to waste any turning the engine over.

Not until he saw if he could get fuel.

The gas station was dark, and it looked as if it had been empty for at least a day. Pops stepped out of the truck, leaving the door open, and I put on the hood of my coat and climbed out.

"Go check on them," Pops said to me as he stared at the pump.

"What do you mean? Check on them?"

"Damn it, George, you know exactly what I mean!"

A slip of the tongue, maybe. He called me "George".

"Just to be clear," I said. "You want me to make sure what? I don't think any got out." I laughed.

"Funny. Just make sure they're all moving back there. Climb up and take a peek."

"Okay." I stepped back.

"Thanks, George."

I paused in walking, looking over my shoulder at Pops. Then I peeked in the cab of the truck. "Ben, I'm checking the back. Making sure they're all moving."

"I'll help." Ben opened the door and got out.

We met up at the back. I could hear the horses and cows.

I noticed how cold it had gotten, and I wanted to rub my hands together. But they just felt weird and dry.

Ben climbed up the back slates. "All the horses are there. Moving."

"How are they not fighting with the cows?" I asked.

"I didn't think cows and horses fight. Besides there's a gate between them. I can't see the cows. I'll go up the side."

"Thanks. Hey, Ben …"

"Yeah?"

"Pops called…" I was about to tell him when I saw the flashing red and blue lights, along with a "blip-blip" of the quick attention siren.

I turned around to see a police pick-up truck pull behind us.

He left his lights on and stepped out.

The officer wore a raincoat and hat. He was a tall man. He looked like George a little bit.

"You kids aren't alone, are you?" he asked.

"Our grandfather…"

Before I could answer fully, Pops came from the front. "Afternoon, Officer."

"You folks stuck?" he asked. "I would have thought it was abandoned had I not seen the two red coats. Three now."

"We're almost out of fuel," Pops said. "Was hoping for a miracle here. Trying to get my pot to the government transport."

"Teetersville?" he asked.

"Yes, Sir," Pops replied.

The officer whistled. "Still have forty miles." He peered up. "They're saying a storm is coming. Not sure what all that will entail. Tell you what: If you feel like detouring six miles out of your way, South, then southwest, there's tankers out at the Municipal airport filling up buses and trucks. I can radio ahead for you."

Pops exhaled loudly. "Oh, that would be fantastic! And I'd be grateful." He held out his hand to the officer. "Really kind of you, Officer…"

"Bill. Just call me Bill. And get those kids to safety. That will be thanks enough. Drive defensive and drive slow."

"We will. You get to safety as well," Pops told him.

"I plan to evacuate tomorrow. Just making sure everyone gets through," he said.

I looked to the policeman. "Thank you, Officer Bill."

He nodded and gave directions to Pops; then got back into his truck as we loaded in ours.

"I checked the back. We checked the back," I told Pops. "Like you asked."

"Huh?" Pops asked confused. "I asked you to check the back." He shook his head and put the truck in gear. "I must not have been paying attention."

"Probably," I said.

"Let's fuel up so we don't have to John Wayne the load," Pops pulled out.

The idea of getting fuel made me feel better. Anything that would get us to the next destination faster was fine by me.

Finding the airport was easy, and it didn't take long.

A series of backroads took us there where we saw a long line of trucks, buses, and other large vehicles waiting in line to get fuel from the four tankers parked there.

Thirty minutes into waiting, Pops shut off the engine. He didn't want to take a chance of running out of fuel completely.

It was then, I started realizing how cold it was. Even more so when Pops got out of the truck to get directions back to the highway.

Pops not having a map surprised me since he had given us

local maps.

My eyes kept shifting to Pops as he spoke to some man.

"Ben? Do you think Pops is okay?" I asked.

"Why are you asking?"

"He called me 'George'."

"Well, George called me Marty several times when we were packing up to move. I wouldn't worry about that."

I wasn't one hundred percent honest with my brother. It was a little more than Pops calling me the wrong name. I shucked it off as worry.

Pops' door opened, and he rushed inside.

"My God, it's cold." He shivered and made a vocal "brr". "Alright. So, we aren't too far off. We'll keep going on this road, and that should lead us to Three-Eighty-Five, mile marker seventeen; which is about twelve miles from where we need to be."

"Now we just need gas," I said.

"We'll be there in an hour." Pops patted my knee as reassurance. Then, like me, he jumped a little, startled by the loud crack of thunder.

The thunder continued, roaring as if it never was going to stop.

I leaned forward to peer out the windshield. The sky grew dark, really dark and super fast. "Pops?"

"Don't worry. Look." Pops smiled. "We're up. We'll be on the road and in Teetersville before this thing even hits."

"Are you sure?"

Pops nodded. "Positive." He turned over the engine, it sputtered some, but it overturned enough to moved us forward to the tanker that would fill us up.

TWENTY-SEVEN – FOLDED

When Officer Bill said, "There's a storm coming. I didn't know what all that entails…" I don't think anyone did.

A massive volcanic eruption, one that would change the face and temperature of the earth. It certainly would cause aftershocks of devastation.

It made sense.

We weren't but a couple miles from the airport when it suddenly went from day to black hole night.

The only specks of light were the flashes of violent lightning. It was a strobe light in the cab of the truck. Rods of electrical light, huge, fired across the sky. Some behind the thick cloud, causing them to look red.

Thunder, lightning; continuous without a break.

Pops called it an electrical storm. He kept driving, barely batting an eye.

"Just lights and noise," he said. "Nothing more. A noisy lightshow."

It was the first time since everything happened that Pops was wrong.

Gusts of wind soon joined the noisy lightshow. Blasts of wind so strong it swayed the truck and blew the ash, making it sound like tiny pebbles hitting against the windows and roof.

The animals were scared. I could hear them even over the storm noise. They moved about in the back in a panic, adding to the swaying of the truck.

Then came the rain.

"We're almost at the highway," Pops said. "We have to be. Once we're off these country roads, we'll be good. Roads are clear of traffic. We'll be good."

I didn't say anything. Neither did Ben.

I looked at my brother who stared forward, never once looking back at me.

I tried to read him. But reading Ben was always difficult, even under the best circumstances. Sometimes his face was so emotionless, it was hard to tell if he was happy, sad, or scared.

Ben didn't look confident or scared. He just looked blank.

I needed him to give me something. As much as I believed Pops, he was trying to protect us, keep us from getting frightened.

Ben didn't have that fake filter. He pretended for no one, because he just wasn't able to.

"You okay, Ben?" I asked.

Ben didn't answer.

A flash of light, brightening the cab, gave me the answer.

He wasn't. He was scared. He didn't need to say it or show it, his hands held onto the handle of the door tight enough to give me my answer.

At first it was just blackness. The headlights reflecting off the fast-falling ash. No indication of which way the road was going. I don't know how Pops did it. How could he see? He drove slowly.

"Two miles," Pops said. "Two miles. Did you see the sign? Two miles to Three-Eighty-Five."

Would being on a highway make a difference?

Pops projected so.

Then it started to rain.

At first, it was a drizzle, then typical rain. It made Pops laugh.

"Here we go," he said. "This should make it better."

He turned on the wipers, clearing the view.

I thought it would be for the best. The rain would wash away all the ash.

As the rain fell harder, I soon learned a flood of volcanic ash became a thick, tar-like mud.

We drove through chocolate fudge. That was how it felt.

"The highway is just a little ahead," Pops announced.

I could feel the wheels fighting to get through the sludge. The rain mixed with the ash as it fell from the sky, coating the windshield. And the wipers did nothing.

Flashes of light. Claps of thunder. Cattle going insane. Horses sounded off erratically.

All while the wipers just smeared the onslaught of what came from the sky.

I didn't know how Pops did it.

Maybe the highway would be better.

"Almost, almost," Pops told us. "We just need to make miles. Every mile south we go, the farther we get. The better it will get."

The truck slowed down, and it wasn't anything that Pops did. The tires spun as they fought to make any traction.

"Look," Pops said. "There's the highway turn."

The headlights cast enough light through the falling mud to brighten the highway entrance sign.

Not that I knew anything about driving or controlling a vehicle, especially one as big as the bull rack. But it had to be the worst combination of timing.

Storm raging, Pops cautiously eased into his turn when the huge crash and thump happened mid-turn.

The sound was loud, exploding through the cab of the truck. Something hit us. It was so heavy that it caused the back end to swerve out of control. And that, in turn, caused the front end to sway left to right.

If the ash mud wasn't so thick, it would have been worse. It held us back even as the truck slid through it.

I never knew cows could scream. They made such an ungodly noise. A horrible background soundtrack to it all.

Pops hugged that wheel, trying to bring the truck back under control.

It was useless.

I couldn't see what was happening, but I only could guess the back rack was swinging out again, causing us to do a complete one-eighty. And we slid backwards slightly diagonal until we came to a halt.

Ben looked in shock, breathing heavily and not blinking.

Pops looked out his window, his back to me. "Okay. Take a breath. Hoods up. Grab your bags and step out."

"You want us to get out of the truck in this weather?" I asked, panicked.

"Yes, you need to go."

Ben reached down to his feet. Lifting his backpack and the "light" bag, he opened the door, looked at Pops, and climbed out.

"Now you," Pops said.

"But Pops…"

"Marty, go!"

What did he see out that window? Did he see anything? How could he? It was so dark and rainy. I grabbed my stuff and slid to the door.

"Marty," Pops called my name calmly. "We're real close to the edge of the road. Looks like part of the guardrail is washed away. I'm gonna try to move the truck. If something happens…"

"Pops, no."

"Just keep going. It's only twelve miles. Back away once you get out."

Nervously, I nodded my agreement and stepped from the truck.

I didn't expect to sink into the ground.

The ash mud mixture came to my shins. I felt how cold it was, seeping into my shoes. It was horrible; but at least the rain slowed down. The time between the thunder and lightning increased.

Ben stood a good ten feet away, on the other side of the road.

With the rain slowing down, it wasn't as dark; and I could see the black rain landing on my coat. The animals were loud.

I shifted my eyes from my sleeve to the backend of the bull rack. I wasn't sure, but it looked like blood, rolling down the side. It could have been the rain, an optical illusion. I fumbled for the flashlight in my raincoat pocket and shined it on the truck. Immediately, the beam caught the wide-open eyes of a cow. The entire top had folded from the weight of a tree, or at least a large branch that crashed down. The cow was dead.

Those poor animals. I felt sick for them. No wonder they were scared and crying out.

"It's not raining as bad. We should have stopped earlier," I said.

"No." Ben said. "If it wasn't this, it would have been something else. We never would have got through. Look."

He moved his flashlight, and I followed the beam. Behind us was just crushed with trees. And, though it was hard to see, the road looked torn up.

"Come on, Pops," Ben said softly.

The wheels of the truck spun loudly.

Like with the rain, my thoughts went to maybe Pops should wait. The thick mud felt like it was receding. It pulled like the current of an ocean.

"Why doesn't he just unload the animals here?" I asked. "Instead of moving the truck."

"Because the road collapsed, Marty," Ben replied. "Where do you think the mud is running to?"

I walked around to the front of the truck to see. I'd only be there a second, but I needed to see how close Pops was to the edge.

I stepped into the headlight beams.

"Marty!" Pops yelled. "Get out of the way!"

For that moment, he stopped spinning the tires.

All I could think was *Oh my God!* From what I could see, the wheels were so close. Pops knew that. He saw that and made up the story about the guardrail because I didn't see a guardrail.

I jumped out of the way, dragging my feet as fast as I could through the mud. As soon as I cleared the way, Pops caught a break, and the truck launched forward. Enough to get traction and move the bull rack.

It caused the animals to squeal louder.

Pops moved it until the wheels spun again, and then he stopped.

The back end looked too close to the edge of the road. Maybe Pops knew that but needed to tend to his livestock. Get the truck far enough to put down the ramp.

The noises they made scared me. They sounded wild.

Pops pulled out a large spotlight and neared the side of the back. He shone the light in, "Looks like we lost two. Okay…" he turned around. "I need you both out of the way. Stand by the front end of the truck where it's safe. They're going to rush out, and it could be dangerous."

"Pops," Ben said. "Let me help."

"No. Not at all. Now, get! Get to the front. These animals are scared, and they're too big for you to be in their way."

Ben and I went to the front end. I stood near the driver's side to see Pops, to watch him.

There was so much sludge, Pops had a hard time moving. Maybe when the animals charged out, they would be hindered by the mud on the road.

"Easy, easy," Pops called out.

The animals sensed him, heard him, and the back end shook as they tried to get out.

They were already charging, and the back gate wasn't even down.

Pops stood by the driver's side near the back. His feet slipped so near the edge of the washed out road, my heart skipped a beat every time I saw it.

But he had to be there to unlatch the gate and let it drop.

He kept telling them, "Easy," but they didn't understand. How could they understand?

The storm had quieted down for a few minutes. So, when a loud, unexpected blast of thunder rang out, it startled them all.

It startled me as well. But it was nothing compared to what it did to the animals.

I couldn't see them. But by hearing the horses, I imagined them on hind legs, bucking some in fear. The cows rushing into each other.

The entire slatted back end jolted. And Pops, like he was some sort of superhero, held up his hand.

Perhaps he thought he was strong enough to hold it back. His hand on the already weakened slats didn't do any good.

The back ramp dropped. The road beneath his feet gave way at the same time as the driver's side wooden slats of the bull rack collapsed. The rear portion cracked previously from the tree limb, folded at the weight of the panicked animals.

Pops tried to hold on and gain a footing. But a horse, fleeing for its safety, brushed into Pops a split second before he was pummeled by one of his cattle.

I watched as Pops, along with not only a portion of the back end, but two cows, tumbled with the crumbling earth.

TWENTY-EIGHT – NO CHOICE

"Pops!" I screamed. It felt as if it happened in slow motion. Watching him fall silently. My scream took every ounce of my breath to produce. "Pops!" I rushed forward, but Ben stopped me.

"You have to watch. The road may give again."

"He's out there. He's down there, Ben. Oh my God."

"Marty, calm down. This isn't helping him."

"We can't leave him."

"We're not. We have to walk around the truck."

My brother was right. The driver's side of the back end was pure wreckage.

Ben grabbed my hand and led me to a safe spot. I just kept looking at the back end, hearing the remaining animals crying inside.

When we arrived at the back, Ben swung the light bag around and reached in. He pulled out a spotlight. "Here. Stay back but look down to see if you see him. Okay?"

"Okay." I nodded, then saw him walking up the back ramp. "What are you doing?"

"Look for Pops. I have to let the load out. I have to ease the weight so the truck is stable. We don't need it tumbling down or causing more road to collapse."

"Can that happen?"

"I don't know." Ben shook his head. "Just look for Pops. As soon as I let them out, I'll help you."

I nodded and realized at that moment, on the side of the dark road, there was really nowhere safe. I just had to hope I could spot Pops without falling down the roadside. Hope that Ben didn't get crushed by the herd when he let them out.

My hands shook, and my fingers fumbled to turn on the handheld spotlight. Specks of light rain and ash floated in the beam of light as I cast it down the hill.

It was like searching an abyss. So dark and vast. A few clumps of crumbled highway would come into my scope.

"Pops!" I cried out. "Pops!"

I heard a rustling sound and a cow groaning out a painful sound. I tried to look for it; but it was drowned out by the sound of the cattle being freed from the back end. The clumping sound of hooves on the wooden ramp, as all of them called out. I wouldn't even call it moos because they sounded like cries.

"Pops!" I screamed, trying to be louder than the cattle.

Then my beam caught movement below.

A shuffling. Had the light not reflected in the cow's eyes, I wouldn't have found my searching spot.

The cow shook his head. And after a few attempts and struggles, it made it to its feet. When it did, I saw a spot of red in the sea of black.

Pops.

My concern was more than Pops falling with the crumbling road, it was also the cows that went with him. They were a thousand pounds at least. He preached how dangerous they could be, and I was scared to death because I didn't see Pops moving.

"I see him, Ben!" I cried out. "I see his red coat."

"How far down?"

"I don't know."

Ben stood next to me.

"Do you see him?" I asked.

"Yeah. I'll get the rope."

I did a double take to ask Ben why he needed one. It wasn't that steep, and we certainly weren't using it to drag Pops over the rocks.

Unless...

Ben returned with the rope and immediately crouched down to the rear tire, reaching under it.

"Ben, why do we need a rope?" I asked. "It's not steep."

"It might be slippery," Ben replied. "And I'll need it as a guide. Plus, if Pops… if Pops is…" he paused. "We're not leaving him down there."

"He's not."

"He's not moving or responding."

"He's not dead!" I shouted.

"Fine. Hold onto the rope to make sure my knot doesn't loosen." Ben stood, then tossed the looped rope down the collapsed road. "I won't put pressure on it unless I need to."

"You're going down?"

"Yeah."

I shook my head. "No. You're stronger than me. I'll go down. You hold the rope."

"Marty, I don't think you should."

"I want to. Hold the rope and the light. I have one too."

"Okay… just hold on. Please."

My gloves were wet, and I worried about them slipping on the rope, so I didn't want to rely on it too much. I used it more as my guide as I stepped down that first rock step.

That was the hardest one. It was a drop about three feet but seemed like more in the dark since it was hard to judge depth perception.

I kept my light on Pops, wishing with every step I took that I would see him move.

"Pops," I called his name. "Pops!"

The cow groaned out, and with the sound of falling rocks, the animal was in my beam of light making its way up over the rocks.

My heart dropped as it ran right to me.

Immediately, I crouched down, covered my head, and put my back to it, fearful it would bulldoze over me.

I felt it brush as it gained its footing and rushed toward Ben.

"Ben!" I hollered. "Are you okay?"

"Yeah, are you?"

"I'm fine." I slipped some as I stood up. It wasn't steep. It was uneven and covered in a layer of slushy ash.

When I aimed my light back down toward Pops, I gasped when he sat up.

"Pops!" I yelled out excitedly.

"Stay there, Marty. I'll be alright."

I always listened to Pops but didn't at that moment. Instead, I ran to him.

It was hard to see his face. The hood of the poncho shadowed it, and it was covered with dirt.

"Is he okay?" Ben yelled.

"He's alive."

It didn't take me long to get to him. Only a few seconds. When I arrived, Pops was sitting up, he was slightly turned with his hand on the head of a cow that lay next to him.

Pops let out a soft, saddened "Aw" and shook his head. "Poor girl." Another shake of his head, and he looked at me. "Poor girl."

"Pops," I gushed and dropped down to my knees by him. "Are you okay?"

"Not sure. Everything kinda hurts. Then again, at my age, it doesn't take much to do that."

I reached down for him, and the beam from my flashlight moved over his face. I saw blood mixed in with the dirt. "Pops, can you walk?"

"You really think you can help me up?" he asked. "You're an itty bitty thing."

"I'm stronger than I look."

Very seriously, he looked at me. "Yes. You are."

"I was worried. You didn't answer."

"I couldn't. That steer was on my leg. And with one startle, he could have trampled me. Sorry I scared you."

"I'm just glad you're alive. Here." I handed him the rope. "It's not all me. Ben has the other end."

"Good. We'll work together." Using the rope and relying some on me, Pops stood. Something was wrong. His one leg immediately gave out, and he hunched forward some, like he had a belly ache. I could feel his arms tense and heard the soft painful grunt he tried to hide from me.

"Do you want me to get Ben to help?"

"No. No." Pops shook his head. "We got this. I can do this." He exhaled slow and heavily, glancing up to Ben. "We can do this. I'm fine."

But really… he wasn't.

<><><><>

In the minutes it took for me and Pops to join Ben, the damp ash that had mixed with rain stopped, and the dry ash fell once more.

"Looks like snow," Pops said holding out his hand. "How many did we lose? Wanderers and killed. How many?"

I shook my head.

"I didn't check," Ben replied.

"Could you count for me, Ben?" Pops asked as he grabbed the back end of the truck for support. "I would like to know."

"Yes, sir," Ben answered. "Can we get you situated, please?"

"I'm fine."

"Pops, please?" Ben asked.

"Yep." Pops sighed out as he looked down. "Yeah, this truck is going nowhere. Wheel's all crooked. Axle's probably busted."

Pops was wrong about the truck going nowhere. I knew we needed to get him out of the ash, cleaned up, and check out how badly he was injured.

The only safe place was inside the cab of the truck.

With the weight of the animals out from the back, it stood less of a chance of causing the road to crumble more. The fast-falling ash gave a little traction. And while we still couldn't drive it, I was able to move the truck another twenty feet or so from the side and more to the center.

Enough so it was safe.

We had Pops take off his poncho outside the truck, and Ben

and I helped him into the passenger side. We reclined that portion back as far as it would go and turned the overhead cab light on to see.

It was cramped with both of us trying to be nurses to Pops.

Using bottled water, I cleaned off his face. He had some gashes on him. One on his nose, another on his cheek, and an abrasion on his forehead.

They were minor compared to his other injuries.

His left pant leg was bloody around the shin, and we knew it wasn't just broken. The bone popped clean through.

How he wasn't screaming in pain, I didn't know.

He talked a bit out of breath and said his side "ached" him some. We lifted his shirt, and when we did, we saw a huge purple spot that covered the entire left side of his belly.

"Get me the black duffel bag from the back," Ben told me.

I reached behind the seat, pulling forth the bag that had our food.

Ben opened the passenger door, stepped out, and from outside, adjusted that bag on the floor of the passenger side.

"Hey, Pops," he said. "Your leg is broke. I have to move it to prop it up. Okay?"

"Yeah. That's fine."

"Pops has another poncho in the back, Marty," Ben told me. "Can you grab that for me? I'll be back."

"Where are you going?"

"I'll be right back," Ben replied.

"Count them heads!" Pops ordered.

Again, I went behind the seat and found the poncho. It wasn't red, it was black. I opened the package and pulled it out.

Ben was gone a few minutes and he returned with a piece of wood that had broken off the back. "Did you get that poncho?"

I handed it to him. "Here."

"Pops, this is gonna hurt; okay?" Ben said. "I have to splint your leg. I don't know if I'll do it right."

"At that angle you can't do it yourself." Pops sat up. "Put the board under my leg. Marty, you hold it there."

Nodding, I slid down from the seat. Ben put the board in place, and I held his leg steady.

"Hold it tight," Pops said. "Ben, string that poncho under and get ready to tie it fast and hard. Got that?"

"Yes, sir."

"Ready?" Pops looked at me. "Hold it tight."

"Okay," I replied nervously, not knowing what he was going to do.

Pops slowly reached down to his injured leg. He tentatively hovered his hand over the wound. "Ben, how many do I have left? Did you count?"

"I did. Four horses and a steer ran off. We lost four cattle."

"Down to eight and twenty-five. Not bad. Let's do this."

Do what? I wondered.

Pops gave a count of three, took a deep breath, and with a one, two, three, he extended his leg and pushed down hard on the bone that stuck out.

He grunted loud and painfully. I felt the pain for him. I wanted to scream.

Ben tied the poncho over the wound, wrapped it around, and tied it again.

"Good," Pops groaned out breathless. "That's good. That's good." He exhaled and sat back. "Marty, get me my whiskey."

In all the years I had known Pops, I saw him drink whiskey twice. A beer maybe at a picnic. Never the hard stuff. The bottle was old and three quarters full. I was sure he brought it for nostalgia reasons, never thinking he would need it for anything else.

"Are you warm enough, Pops?" I lifted a blanket. "Let me cover you."

"That's enough fussing over me. I'm just gonna rest."

I brought the blanket over him.

"Marty," Ben said still standing outside, "Can I talk to you?"

"Yeah. I'll be back, Pops." I kissed him on the cheek.

Ben shut the passenger door, remaining outside, and I exited through the driver's door, meeting him out there.

If I knew or had experienced a snowstorm, I would know for sure that was what it looked like with the falling ash.

The animals were all in the road. Moving about in no particular order. Just in circles, confused and scared.

"Marty, Pops is bad," Ben said. "I mean, I don't know. But he needs help."

"Do you think we can get him on a horse?"

Ben chuckled sadly. "No. And even if we could, look at the horses."

I did. The storm and crash had rattled them to the point that they seemed wild, untamed.

"What do we do? Maybe unhitch the back…?"

"No." Ben shook his head. "I'm gonna go find help."

"What?" I lost my breath. "No."

"Marty, I have to. There's no choice. I'll walk and find help. It's twelve miles. You heard Pops. Teetersville is not that far." Ben walked over to the truck where his backpack rested against the front wheel.

At first, I wondered what it was doing there. Then I remembered Pops made us take them out of the truck right after the crash. Our backpacks from camp; they had our supplies.

"I don't want to tell Pops. Let him rest," Ben said. "Let him have his drink for pain. But make sure he gets water. You, too." Ben put on his pack. "Start the truck every thirty minutes to keep the battery charged and for heat."

"Ben. Please. No. Don't go. It's dark. The ash…"

"I'll stay straight on this road. I'll be careful. It's the only way. Marty…" He stepped to me. "We can't let him die. We have to try to get him help. He would do the same for us. Stay with him. Take care of him."

I grabbed my brother and wrapped my arms around him so tight. I fought back the tears. "My whole life," I spoke as I squeezed him. "I felt like the older sister. I knew I wasn't. I felt it. But right now, I know for sure I'm not. I am so proud to call you my big brother."

"I love you."

I whimpered and sniffed. "Love you, too, Ben."

Ben stepped from the embrace. "I'll be back with help."

He looked at me once, then started walking. He stayed close to the truck until he cleared the animals, and I saw the flashlight turn on.

My brother had been protected his whole life; guided and told what to do. Him walking alone, down an ash-covered highway in the dark, in a strange place, was of his own doing. His own choice.

It was a huge step and undertaking.

In a way, he was still being guided. But this time, by his desire to protect and help.

I was scared to death for him. Scared for me. He was my brother. I needed him and prayed he would get to Teetersville safely.

I stayed on the road until I couldn't see Ben or his light any longer. Then, I made my way back to the truck to be with Pops.

TWENTY-NINE
– IT'S OKAY

Before Pops could take another drink of whiskey from his bottle, I made him sip some water.

I remembered what Ben had told me, and I knew water was important.

He wouldn't eat, even though I made him some food.

He was being so tough and strong. I wanted to ask him how bad things hurt. But knowing Pops, he'd pretend it didn't.

The cab of the truck needed to be kept as ash-free as possible. It had been two hours since Ben had left. My stomach twitched and turned every time I thought about him out there, walking alone.

Did he see anyone? Was he able to see at all?

A shiver ran up my spine. Not from thoughts about Ben, but from the temperature.

I hadn't turned over the engine. I didn't feel the need to, but it was getting really dark in the truck, and the ash covered the windshield. Plus, I felt it getting cold.

"You okay, Pops?" I asked.

He just looked at me. "How many times are you going to ask me that?"

"I don't know. Are you cold?"

"A little."

"I'll put on the heat."

Reaching for the key to turn on the engine, Pops grabbed my arm, stopping me.

"Before you do that, go check the load," he said.

"I just checked the load an hour ago."

"And you'll check it an hour from now. Go."

"Okay." I grabbed the flashlight and reached for the door handle.

"And when you get back, we'll talk about something else besides my health or comfort."

"Okay." I opened the door, and a gust of wind hit me. It was ash-filled and bitter cold.

The temperature had plummeted. Carefully, I stepped out. Only this time, I didn't sink into a wet, mud-like mixture. It had hardened some, and walking on it was like walking on Jell-o. I could hear and feel it squish beneath my shoes.

The animals were quiet. A few noises here and there. For the most part, they huddled together, probably hungry. I didn't know if they were cold or how long they could take the temperature drop.

I felt horrible for the animals as I counted them. They didn't ask for this. I reminded myself that had we left them behind and not tried to save them, they wouldn't have survived.

Then again, had we left them behind, Pops wouldn't be hurt. And Ben wouldn't be out there walking. Maybe we'd even be near Kansas with my mom, George, and Ruby.

The ranch and animals there were Pops' life. He wasn't leaving it behind without trying to save a part of it.

After I finished counting, I stared out down the road.

It was like seeing a wall of black or the edge of the world. Nothing was out there. The moonless and cloud-covered night sky met with the horizon. And it was difficult to tell where the road ended and the sky began.

Poor Ben. How was he able to walk in that? To navigate?

My heart broke for my brother, thinking about him. Scared to death that he had fallen. Or worse.

"Please, Ben. Be okay," I whispered.

Standing out there for that extra few minutes reminded me how cold it actually was. My fingers felt tingly, and the tip of my nose started to hurt.

I had a truck to retreat to; to warm up in.

Ben didn't.

As if some sort of miniscule sacrifice, I stayed outside in the cold a little longer. For Ben.

It was strange. I knew that. And eventually I went back to the truck.

I took off my coat as I opened the door and shook it off.

Not that it made that much of a difference. Just as much ash blew in during that open-door timeframe than if I just got inside covered in ash.

"Did we lose more?" Pops asked.

"No. Why?"

"You were out there a while."

"I was... I was staying out there to get cold."

"Why?"

"For Ben. Because I know he's not warm," I replied. "It's silly, I know."

"It's your brother."

I turned over the engine and immediately turned on the windshield wipers to clear the ash.

Pops joked and said, "That won't last."

"I know." I reached my hand for the vent. The air coming out wasn't warm yet.

Pops grunted as he sat up some. "You should have gone with him."

"Why would I do that?"

"So you both could be somewhere safe in twelve miles."

"Who would look after you?" I asked.

"Oh, I'm tough. I'd be fine."

"Yeah, you would be. But who would check the animals?"

"You have a point."

"Plus," I said. "I wanted to stay with you. If it wasn't for you, Pops, who knows where me and Ben would be? You gave us that bug-out bag stuff, along with a map. You also came looking for us."

"That's what grandfathers do. Grandparents go that extra little mile just to annoy your folks." Pops turned some and faced me. "Marty, in all seriousness, I'm…. I'm proud of you and Ben. Really, really proud of you two. You've done really good. You're gonna be okay in this world."

When he said that, immediately I saw Jean Jacket Man's face and my head lowered.

"What is it?" he asked.

"Pops, can I tell you something?"

"Sure you can."

"I did something bad," I said. "Really, really bad."

"When?" he asked.

"After we left Bigfoot Camp on the way to the state line. And I am telling you not because I want you to do that grownup thing and tell me it's alright. I'm telling you because I need… I need to tell someone older."

"You told Ben?"

I nodded.

"What did he say about this bad thing?" Pops asked.

"Nothing."

"Well, that's your brother for you. The strong, silent type."

"Yeah, he really doesn't talk about it," I said.

"Things have a way of registering differently with your brother. What did you do, Marty?"

"I can't stop thinking about it, Pops." I grabbed his hand. "I can't. I feel horrible…"

"Marty…"

"I killed someone."

Pops immediately widened his eyes, as if his attention was suddenly caught. "What?"

"On the way from camp, a man attacked Ben. He was beating him and hurting him. A *man*, Pops. A grown man was beating Ben."

"That's how he got the black eye and messed up cheek?"

I nodded. "I tried to stop him. I yelled, screamed, fought him; but I couldn't stop him. I had a knife, and I stabbed him."

Pops squeezed my hand.

"And I couldn't stop," I started crying. "I couldn't stop stabbing him. I don't know why I couldn't stop. I just kept stabbing him." I sobbed out once, dropping my head to Pops' shoulder.

"Hey, hey." Pops said comforting. "Look at me. Lift your head. Look at me, Marty."

I lifted my head and wiped my hand across my cheek.

"The world is different now. Who knows why we do things? You told me not to tell you it was okay. I won't tell you that. I will say this," Pops said. "You spent your life protecting your brother. Fighting for him. How many scraps have you been in over the years when he was bullied? A... lot." Pops nodded. "You took it to the level it needed to be. It was a big threat, and you protected in a big way."

"It was wrong."

"You did what you had to do," Pops said firm.

"I feel horrible. Horrible and guilty, and I don't want to feel this way."

"Marty, you're human. If you told me you didn't feel bad, then I'd worry. Will you always feel guilty? I think a part of you will when it comes to mind. Horrible?" Pops shook his head. "No. I think you'll stop feeling horrible as you watch this world get pretty bleak."

"He didn't deserve to die," I said. "As bad as he was, as much as Ben didn't deserve to be beat, he didn't deserve to die. I wish I could just say I was sorry."

"Then do it."

"What?"

"Apologize. Say you're sorry."

"What do you mean?" I asked.

"Say it. Say it out loud. Right now."

I hesitated.

"You said you felt guilty. And I say if you didn't get a chance to apologize do it now. Say it..."

"I'm... I'm sorry."

"Louder," Pops instructed.

"I'm sorry!"

"Not to me, to him."

"Pops, he's dead. You mean look for his body?"

Pops laughed. "No. With intention... to him. Put it to the universe, and the universe will deliver the message." He chuckled again, then winced, putting his hand on his gut.

"Pops. I didn't mean to make you hurt..."

"Marty, stop. You didn't make me hurt. You made me smile. Laughter is the best medicine."

"I think they mean medicine for emotions, not physical pain," I said.

"You need to not worry about me. I'll be fine."

"But you're injured."

"Yes. I am. And it hurts pretty bad, too."

"Really?" I asked surprised.

"Don't look so happy."

"That's not it, Pops, it's just... you don't act it. I was worried you had brain damage or nerve damage that didn't let you feel it."

"Oh, I feel it, little one." He grabbed my hand again. "I feel it plenty. But what good is it gonna do me whining in the cab of an old truck to my fifteen-year-old granddaughter? Won't make the pain go away. Now that whiskey... it helps. Give me that bottle back."

After hesitating, I reached for his whiskey, giving him the water before I gave him the alcohol. "Only if you drink this first and eat a couple bites of those crackers."

Pops grumbled. "Fine. Deal. Where are the crackers?"

I reached to the dashboard and pulled the napkin-covered crackers down, handing them to him. "Thank you. I want you better."

"I'll get better." He took a big bite of the cracker, then drank some water. Each swallow looked like it hurt. He gave them back to me. "I will be honest with you. Everything hurts. And I think... while the truck is warming up, I'm gonna close my eyes." He snapped his fingers and pointed to the whiskey.

I watched him take a small drink and put down the bottle.

As he laid back slowly, I brought the blanket over him and kissed him on the cheek. "Get some rest, Pops. Thank you for talking to me."

"We'll talk whenever you want." He closed his eyes, then opened only one. "Oh, and Marty? Don't forget in twenty minutes…"

"In twenty minutes, what?" I asked.

"Check the load." He smiled peacefully and closed his eyes.

THIRTY – CHECK THE LOAD

June 20

It was the complete and utter silence, along with the cold that caused me to wake up with a jump. I had fallen asleep, into a deep sleep in the driver's seat of the truck. I didn't think I would ever sleep. My mind was full, spinning with thoughts of Ben, Pops, my mom, George, and Ruby.

Waking up was worse than trying to fall asleep.

It was so quiet.

It scared me.

No animal noises. No sounds from Pops.

I was afraid to look at him, but I did. His head was tilted toward me, eyes closed.

"Pops?" I called timidly. "Pops. Pops, please."

Softly, and raspy, he spoke, "I'm alive, Marty. If that's what you're worried about."

It was dark in the cab of the truck. I didn't know what time it was until I turned over the engine. The last I had looked; it was four in the morning. Almost twelve hours since Ben had left. When I saw the clock on the radio, I got sick to my stomach.

It was after eight. My brother had been gone sixteen hours.

Something was wrong. I just wanted to cry. In fact, it took everything inside of me not to.

I reached up for the dome light, then for water. "Pops. Do you want water?"

"No."

"You have to have water."

"I will. Let me warm up first."

I knew it would take a while for the truck to heat. It seemed a lot colder than it had been before.

"Sorry about that, Pops," I said. "I fell asleep. I didn't mean to not start the truck."

"I'm not a baby chick that you have to keep warming up. I turned on the truck for a bit when you slept."

"Why is it so cold?"

"Probably colder outside."

I immediately reached for the wipers to clear the ash like I usually did. They didn't move and only made a grinding motor sound. "The wipers are broke."

"They're not broke," Pops replied.

"Listen to them." I turned them on again.

"They're frozen. Whatever is on the windshield is frozen."

I wondered how ash would freeze. Then I remembered it had rained.

I turned them on once more.

"Give it ten minutes, Marty. They'll swipe. But if you don't stop turning them on you will break them."

"Sorry." I removed my hand from the wipers. "I'm from California. I don't know much about the cold stuff."

"You'll learn. It'll be cold, bitter cold, for a while. A lot of ash went up there." Pops shivered. "Is there another blanket?"

"Here, take mine. It's warm." I laid it over him. And when I adjusted the blanket on Pops, my hand touched his arm. "Pops, you're burning up. You have a fever."

"You'll have that."

"No. No you won't have that. Something is wrong."

"Yeah, I got hurt," Pops said. "Of course, something is wrong. A fever is a way to fight off infection."

"Is it the leg?" I asked.

"Probably. My leg was under a dead cow."

I gasped. "Is it like eating rotten meat, only the rotten meat got in your leg."

Pops finally opened his eyes and looked at me. "You did not just say that."

"I don't know. Sorry. I'm scared."

"Marty, don't start panicking," Pops told me.

"I'm not."

"You are."

"Okay, I am."

"Well, stop. Hand me my water please."

I found his bottle of water and gave it to him. "Do you need my help?"

"No. Marty, just…" he struggled and sat up. "Go check the load."

I shook my head.

"Is that a no?"

"I don't want to."

"Because of the cold?" he asked.

"Because I'm afraid."

"Of what?"

"I don't hear the cows or horses. I think they froze to death."

"They may have," Pops said. "But we aren't gonna know unless you go check. Go check."

"Pops."

"Now."

I grabbed my raincoat and put it on. Not that it would keep me warm, but I wasn't going to be outside very long. My insides shook. I didn't want to go out there and see the dead animals. Seeing them would make me worry more about Ben.

I put on the hood, then my gloves, reached for the handle, opened the door, then immediately shut it.

"What is it?" Pops asked.

"It's not dark. I mean, it's not bright, but it's not dark anymore."

"Good. You can see where you're going. Check the load."

I opened the door and the cold air blasted me long with a gust of… snow.

It had snowed.

Pops was right. I was able to see. I wasn't sure I wanted to.

It definitely was daylight. The sky was gray, a dark gray. I couldn't see the sun. But I was sure it was up there because there was finally some light.

It reminded me of twilight. That moment just before the sun set, only without the pretty colors of orange.

Snow had accumulated a few inches on the running boards of the truck and, when I stepped down, it made its way into my shoe. It was cold and I could feel it against my sock.

I didn't want to fall so I was careful as I stepped down. There was a soft layer of snow, but the ground was frozen beneath it.

I turned around and looked at the truck. It was covered in snow.

The gusting, frigid wind blocked out all sounds.

I didn't want to walk around the other side of the truck to check the load because I was sure they were all dead.

Not having the best shoes for snow walking, I moved around the front of the truck, holding on so as not to fall.

With each step I took, I grew more and more frightened of what I'd see. Until I made it around the truck.

They weren't all dead.

Numerous clouds of steam carried in the falling snow from the warm breath of the animals.

They didn't move much. Some huddled close. Others were picking at the broken back end of the bull rack for hay.

The farther into the road I walked, the deeper the snow was.

Between the snow and the steam, it was hard to see them good enough to count, but I tried. I was excited to tell Pops they were still alive.

For how long?

I had to think of another plan. It was lighter out. Maybe it was time for me to walk and get help.

Unlike the night before, the horses were calmer. There was no way Ben could have taken one, especially since he never rode. Neither had I; but it would be easier with a calmer horse.

I could take one and ride the twelve miles.

Find my brother.

Get Pops help.

That's what I would do.

I had to restart my count, and when I got to the sixth horse, I heard the beep of a horn.

I panicked.

Pops was beeping for me. A muffled beep from a horn buried in snow.

Hurriedly, I turned to race back to the truck.

Beep-beep-beep.

I stopped.

It wasn't coming from our truck. Slowly, I looked over my shoulder and saw them.

Two sets of headlights cutting through the snow.

One bigger and higher than the other set.

I ran toward them; they weren't moving very fast.

Clearly one was a truck. The other, a car or SUV.

Did they see us? I hoped so. The cows scattered from the horn blasting, and the horses moved as well.

I waved my hands high in the air. They had to see me in that red coat. They had to.

"Help!" I shouted. "Help us."

More than likely, they didn't hear me. But I knew for sure they saw me. I was caught in the dim headlights of the car.

It stopped, and the truck stopped right behind not far from where the animals made their snow-covered pasture.

I could make out the outline of the vehicles. Everything was still colorless, even with the snow. The one wasn't a car it was a Humvee.

The Humvee doors opened at the same time, and two figures stepped out.

"Marty!"

When I heard the call of my name, my knees buckled.

"Ben!" I cried out.

It was my brother. He made it.

Ben also brought help.

THIRTY-ONE – HITCHIN' A RIDE

Two men ran by me before I even met up with my brother. They carried a big red box with a white cross on it.

And they ran directly to the truck.

"I told them Pops was in there."

"Thank you. Thank you so much," I said.

"I'm sorry it took so long," Ben had said. "Please tell me Pops is okay."

"He's alive," I replied. "Dictating. But he isn't doing good."

Ben explained how he walked a long time and had to stop a lot because he veered off the road. Even with the flashlight it was hard to see. As the night rolled on, the weather grew colder, and the thick ash-fall made it nearly impossible to see.

He didn't know how far he was from Teetersville.

"If it wasn't for the red poncho," Ben explained. "Two soldiers making a town sweep wouldn't have spotted me walking. They gave me a ride, but they had to finish their work. Funny. We couldn't see anything ahead. Then we spotted you in the red coat."

"Pops and the red coats," I told him. "He did it on purpose."

"Anyway, they got me to Teetersville, and that was a whole mess. No one believed me. It was like they kept saying to 'step aside'. They were dealing with patients from some big accident on Interstate Eighty."

"Big accident?"

Ben nodded. "Yeah. Bunch of people evacuating to Kansas

City."

"Is that the way Mom and George would go?" I asked.

"I don't know. But it didn't just happen, though. Happened a couple days ago. Mom's already in Kansas City. Finally, you aren't gonna believe who saw me."

"Clark?" I asked.

"What? No. Why would you say him? He was headed to Kansas."

I shrugged. "I just figured he was the person who would pop up unexpectantly and help."

Ben grumbled. "Hmm. Well, we know how well he helped last time. Anyhow, Officer Bill."

"The policeman that helped us get gas?"

Ben nodded. "And you know how he recognized me?"

"The red poncho."

"Yep. It's crazy. Anyhow…" Ben shifted his eyes to the truck.

I thought something was wrong, and I looked as well. The two medical people were talking to Pops, giving him instructions.

"Sorry. Anyhow," Ben continued. "I was worried, you know. Remember how I wondered if Pops was right or wrong? Maybe he wasn't thinking clearly about the government transport?"

"Yeah, I do. But there is a government transport. We know that was true."

"Yep. I was worried when Officer Bill walked me over. The government guy looked perturbed and then turned out to be really nice. Pops was on the list. That's how we got the big rack."

I hadn't even thought about it until Ben said that. The other vehicle was a huge truck. Three men has stepped out to assess the livestock.

"Ben. They aren't gonna steal them. Are they?"

Ben shook his head. "I don't think so. The government guy said he'd talk to us after we got Pops the help he needed."

"Do they have doctors there?"

"I guess. Marty, I don't know. I was just happy to get you guys help and was so worried I was too late."

"I was worried about you," I said. "I was getting ready to come for you."

"You probably would have made it easier than me now that there's some light."

"Did you ask about Mom or anyone from Chadron?"

"No," Ben replied. "I didn't have time to do that. I just was trying to get help. We can ask anything when we get there. I don't know if people will have the answers. But we can try."

I nodded, arms folded tight, and accepted that.

Ben found help. That was what mattered at that moment.

With Ben next to me, we walked to the truck where the two medics were working on getting Pops out of the truck.

"Do you need help?" I asked.

"Marty," Pops said. "We're fine."

The one medic looked at me. I couldn't see his mouth; but by his eyes, I knew he was smiling. "Is he always like this? Stubborn?"

"Yes. But tough," I replied.

"He is. He had to be to survive this," the medic replied. "We got here in the nick of time."

Pops blurted out. "Quit scaring her and being melodramatic. I had a good few hours left in me."

The medic pointed back. "Just so you know: Once we get him in the Humvee, I'm knocking him out."

I didn't know if the medic was joking or not. I think he saw my confusion.

"He needs to be sedated so he stays still," the medic explained.

"Oh. Okay. Thank you."

"We will be a few more minutes. Then, we'll all load up and go."

"What about the animals?" I asked.

"They'll get them," the medic replied. "Your grandfather is our number one concern."

I stepped back out of their way to watch.

Ben put his hand on my back. "He's getting help. He'll be

fine."

I hoped Ben was right. Pops had to get better. He had to be fine.

Ben and I didn't know where our mother was, or George or our sister.

Pops was all we had at that moment. And we couldn't lose him.

THIRTY-TWO – WAITING

Teetersville, NE

I had never been to or heard of Teetersville. The medic in the Humvee called it a one stoplight town.

Before the eruption, I imagined it looked differently. Maybe a lot like Chadron. The cute towns you see in movies.

There was no way there were tents and trailers set up in the middle of Main Street all the time.

It reminded me of a street fair.

The town still had power and strings of lights ran down both sides of the street. Fires were lit in cans.

When we left in the Humvee, they were still loading the animals in the new truck. That truck was huge, with plenty of room for the horses.

I never saw them finish. We drove slow on the snow-covered roads. A few times I felt the Humvee slide; but the driver never flinched.

Once we arrived in town, one of the medics quickly retrieved a rolling cart, and they placed Pops on it. It that short span of time, Pops was no longer speaking or griping. I hoped it was whatever medicine they gave him and not something worse.

We wanted to follow and go with Pops, but one of the medics said we couldn't.

"Listen: He needs a doctor fast," the medic said. "He'll need surgery, I can tell you that. His leg is… bad. He has what I think is a hemothorax."

"What's that?" I asked.

"Bleeding in and around the lungs. Probably from the broken ribs. But to be honest, I'm more worried about the leg right now. He's in a good place. They have a hack of a trauma set up here."

He directed us to an art gallery. He said it was four shops down on the right. It was the designated waiting place for anyone new in town.

"It's warm," he said. "Wait there. We'll know where to find you about your grandfather and any other check-in procedure."

What choice did we have but to go to this art gallery? I couldn't help but feel somehow Ben and I were going to get lost in the shuffle. How could we not? There were so many people moving about. Some in uniforms, some wearing protective clothing.

The only thing I really needed was a new mask. Ben had gotten a new one. Mine was filthy and heavy.

It didn't feel as cold as we walked down the sidewalk. It snowed but I think the fire cans—everything was tight and blocked in—along with the fact there was power, kept it from getting as cold

Four shops down.

An art gallery in a town called Teetersville.

When I thought of an art gallery, I thought of the ones we had in LA or visited in New York when I was twelve. Massive and trendy.

Maybe Teetersville was some hidden gem of art.

Until we arrived.

The handwritten sign on the door read, "Visitors, please leave ash-covered items in vestibule."

"What's a vestibule?" I asked Ben.

"A fancy name for hallway." He pushed open the door. Multitudes of items lined the coat racks and floor.

I didn't want to leave my raincoat. Pops gave it to me. I set it on the floor with my bag on top, hoping neither was stolen.

The inside was long and wide. Vintage with high ceilings.

It actually was an art gallery, and there were dozens of paintings on display. Along with various colorful leather couches and chairs.

It was very... artsy.

Signage on the walls promoted Friday Night open-mic poetry, and Saturdays were single ladies' wine, cheese, and paint nights.

Which probably produced the art hanging on the wall.

There were people in there, and they all stared at us when we walked in.

A woman sat on a blue couch next to a man. She sipped from a mug and set it on the table as we passed her. She glanced up. "Coffee, tea, and food are on the back table, if you're hungry."

"Thank you," I said.

"You two look lost. Are you two waiting for transport? A place to stay?"

Ben looked at the woman. "They told us to wait here. Our grandfather got hurt."

She nodded. "An accident?"

"Yes," I replied.

"That's all there seems to be. Lots of those." She glanced at the man with her. "We thought for sure most issues would be breathing problems from the ash."

"A lot are," he said. "Not as many as the accidents on Eighty. That was big."

The woman shook her head. "We just missed that one. Happened three days ago." She pointed around the room. "Most of these people are waiting for news about a loved one getting treated."

"Are you?" I asked.

"No." She shook her head. "We have a room upstairs. We come down to pass the time."

The man next to her finally spoke. "And be nosey."

"Stop." She nudged him. "We're helpful."

"She's helpful. I just drink my tea." he said. "She's deemed herself social coordinator."

"What else is there to do?" she asked. "Meeting people. I'm Rose, and this is my husband Ron. We're waiting for the government transport. We arrived from Chadron two days ago. It's a long wait."

"Chadron?" I asked. "We came from Chadron. The accident happened moving my grandfather's animals."

She looked at her husband. "Who is your grandfather?"

I was stuck for a second. I drew a blank. I faced Ben. "What's Pops' last name?"

The woman heard me. "Pops McCullen?"

Ben nodded. "Yeah. Bruce is his first name."

"We know him. Everyone calls him Pops. We know him well. We bought my Uncle Bud's stock two years ago. Bud Wheeler. What a small world."

"It *is* a small world," Ben said. "We took your uncle's bull rack."

I don't know why, but that made me snort a laugh.

Rose's smile went from natural to awkwardly forced. "You don't say. Is... uh, is Pops okay?"

"We hope," I replied. "We don't know."

"I'm sure he is. Pops is one tough SOB."

Ben said, "Thank you." Then tugged my arm.

We found the food table in the back. I was hungry and thirsty, and that hot tea sounded good.

I made a cup, along with instant oatmeal, and Ben found us a seat on a red couch that faced a wall of sunflower paintings.

All of them were the same sunflower and vase, all painted differently. Some good. Some bad. Probably done on a wine-and-cheese night as well.

We sat there, slowly sipping our warm beverages, eating oatmeal, and looking at the people who pretended they weren't staring at us.

"McCullen," a male voice called out. "Are the McCullens here?"

Ben and I stood at the same time.

He looked around, spotted us. Then, after nodding once upward, he walked over to us.

He wore a gray protective suit that looked more like coveralls. Clearly he wore a dress shirt and blue tie under. His ash protective face mask was lowered to his chin, and he carried a clipboard.

He wasn't old, but he wasn't young either. Maybe not old enough to have kids my age.

"Aaron Seibert," he shook our hands. "FEMA. Agricultural division. How are you two?"

"Good," Ben answered.

"Wanted to let you know we arrived with the load," he said. "We have…" he looked down to the clipboard. "Quarter Horse count of eight, six steer, and eighteen cattle. Sound right?"

I nodded. "Yes, that was my last count."

"Good." He turned the clipboard over to Ben. "You're the older one? Sign here."

"What is this?" Ben asked.

"Just what we have registered for you."

Rose hurriedly walked over. "Do you mind?" she took the clipboard from Ben's hand and looked over it. "Just checking." She handed it back to Ben. "Go on. Sign. It's just an acknowledgement. Like a receipt."

"We're not giving them to him, are we?" Ben asked.

"No," Rose said. "This just acknowledges what they have in holding for you."

Ben took the pen, hovering it before signing. "What happens next? Do we find out where they're going?"

I had to ask. "Is there any way to find out about our parents?"

Aaron lifted his hand. "I don't know about finding your parents unless they came here."

I shook my head.

"Maybe someone in headquarters can help," Aaron said. "I'm only here for the transport participants. Just sign the receipt."

Ben did. "What now?" He handed back the clipboard.

"Someone will come in to get you a place to stay for the night," Aaron replied.

"No." Ben shook his head. "I mean about all this. The horses. The cattle."

"That depends," Aaron said, then paused. "On what happens with your grandfather." He tucked the board under his arm, thanked us, and walked away.

I stood there stunned.

It depended on what happened with Pops? He said it so nonchalantly. It was as if he were speaking about the weather.

"Will we have baseball practice today?"

"Depends on what happens with the weather."

"Depends on what happens with your grandfather."

It worried me and angered me. It sucked, but there was nothing we could do.

A lot did depend on what happened with Pops.

All we could do was wait.

THIRTY-THREE – REACHING OUT

Pops needed surgery. We were told someone would come to find us when he was out. I asked if we could wait in a waiting room or something, but there wasn't one. The surgery was being performed in a special surgical building brought in for traumatic injuries.

Apparently, there were a lot of injuries, mainly from accidents.

The woman who spoke to us told us that Pops was in the queue and that was a good thing. If he wasn't, he was a lot worse than we wanted him to be. Having to wait his turn meant his injuries more than likely weren't life-threatening.

I liked how she snuck "more than likely" in there.

It didn't make us feel any better.

They gave us a room above the art gallery. It wasn't really a room; more of an apartment where we were given a room.

Other people stayed in that apartment, too. I hadn't seen them. Not that there was anything wrong with that woman, Rose. But she was too up in our business for my liking. So, I hoped it wasn't her in the apartment with us.

It definitely was someone's home before they were evacuated. The beds were made, dishes in the kitchen. But the only food was what they had brought up there for us.

Ben and I would share a bedroom with two twin beds. I was fine with that.

They gave us clothes, but I wouldn't give up my red raincoat.

No way.

I pounded it against the wall outside to remove the ash, like my mom did with the throw rugs to get out dust. Then, I washed it in the big paint sink down in the art gallery.

I forgot how bright it was; and it was after I cleaned it. When I was finished, I stepped out of the back of the gallery and really looked at those who sat in the gallery.

They were on their phones.

Maybe they were using them before; but I was so caught up in the confusion of arriving that I didn't notice. Slowly I walked into the main room.

Did they have a signal or were they just playing games?

I approached a woman who was focusing on her screen, then I saw what it was. "Are you… are you on social media?"

"Yeah." She nodded. "Not much is posted. A few news sites are up."

"The internet is working?" I asked.

"It's spotty."

"The phones?"

"There's service. It's even better east of here."

I sputtered out a "thank you" and took off with my red coat back upstairs.

"Ben!" I shouted as I walked in. "Ben!"

He was in the back bedroom. Sitting up on the bed, he looked at me. "What's wrong?"

"The phones work." I rushed to my backpack.

Ben jumped from the bed and grabbed his. "We have to charge them."

"We have to call mom."

Both of us whipped out our phones and chargers, plugging them in at the same time.

It was like watching a pot of water boil, they just wouldn't charge up.

The plan was simple. He would call George; I would call Mom.

Maybe… just maybe, when they powered up, we'd have a

missed call or text from them. Then again, with the phones being off, we wouldn't see a missed call.

"Four percent," Ben said. "I can make a call."

"Anything from them?" I asked.

He shook his head and started to dial.

"Mine's on," I saw it light up and grabbed it. No missed calls or texts. I hurriedly sought my mom's number.

"Straight to voicemail," Ben said.

I grunted. "Me, too. Try again. But let's leave a message."

Ben nodded.

I got my mother's voicemail. A recording I heard a million times. But this time, it was different. It made me sad to hear her voice. I missed her so much. "Mom," I said. "Hey. It's me." I could hear Ben leaving a message for George. "Ben and I are fine. We hope you're safe. We love you guys. Please tell Ruby I love her. We're with Pops. He got hurt. We're in Teetersville. We're headed with him to Austin to a ranch on July second. That's all I know. Please, get this. Please be safe. I love you."

I hated hanging up, even though it was only a message. I turned to face Ben. He was looking on his phone. "What are you doing?"

"Checking mom and George's profiles. They haven't posted or been on for days."

Posting.

Immediately I went on my own social media. and tagging my mother and George, I posted: "Mom and George, Ben and I are fine. We're in Teetersville. We'll be here until July second. Then heading to Austin."

Surely my mom and George would check social media. I mean, the people down in the art gallery were my parents' age and were on it. They had to know it could be a link to loved ones.

It felt frantic; a rush, as if racing against the clock to get ahold of our mother. Utilizing everything we could think of. It was the first signal in days.

Somehow it felt hopeful.

"Where would they be?" I asked. "Kansas, right?"

"Kansas, yeah," Ben replied. "But they may be on their way to wherever they're sending them."

"Why don't they have a signal?" I questioned. "We have a signal. The woman downstairs said the signal is better out east."

"I don't know. I'm gonna keep trying."

"So will I."

"Marty," Ben said with concern in his voice. "Do you think something is wrong?"

"What do you mean?"

"I mean, we have a signal. In this little town. They took George's car. He has a charger. Even if they did let their phones die, it's been days. We haven't heard anything. Mom would have tried, right?"

I stared at my brother, thinking about what he was implying. A lump formed in my throat.

Our mother... George... They wouldn't just leave and keep going without knowing where we were. I couldn't see them just giving up, not looking for us.

Nothing was wrong.

Maybe they were actually on their way to us.

We were so engrossed that the knock on the door and the call of, "Hello?" of the male voice startled me to the point I nearly screamed.

"Anyone here?" the man called out.

I stepped from the bedroom, into the hall, and peeked into the living room. A man in hospital scrubs stood there.

"I'm looking for the McCullen family," he said.

"That's us," I replied. "Ben!" I called for my brother.

The man shut the door and stepped inside, waiting just in the entranceway until Ben and I were together.

"I'm Captain Carnahan. A doctor, surgeon. Rather, with Emergency Management." He held out his hand.

I shook it, then Ben did.

"Are you Mr. McCullen's grandchildren?" he asked.

I nodded.

"I was looking for you downstairs," he said. "I'm the surgeon who operated on your grandfather."

Immediately I froze, scared to hear what he was going to say.

"I heard you two were with him when he was in the accident?" the doctor asked.

"We were," I answered.

"First, let me tell you: Great job. Honestly, you were the first line of defense, and you held that line," he said. "You saved your grandfather."

"So, he's…"

Doctor Carnahan held up his hand. "He's not out of the woods. He's tough. He is one strong man. He's stabilized now. Do you know what that means?"

I shook my head.

He explained., "It means he's not getting worse, he's… stable. Which, in his condition, is a miracle in itself."

"Can we see him?" I asked.

"Not yet. He's resting. First thing in the morning when the sedative wears off. It would be good to have you there when he wakes. He had internal bleeding, which I believe I was able to stop. And the leg… the leg was really bad. We… I… I wasn't able to save it."

I tilted my head curiously. "What does that mean?"

Ben answered, "They amputated Pops' leg."

"Just…" The doctor said. "From the knee down."

The knee down? Did it really make a difference?

"Do you have any questions?" he asked.

"Does he know?" I asked.

"Not yet. That's why maybe you should be there," the doctor replied. "It was close. Another hour, we would have lost him. I am confident he'll pull through this. Both of you need rest. Are either of you injured? Do you need medical attention?"

Both Ben and I shook out heads.

"Okay, well, just find the medical unit in the morning. I'll be there." He walked to the door and paused. "He's doing better than I would have expected. Hold on to that. I'll see you in the morning."

"Thank you," I said.

The doctor nodded once and walked out.

Ben and I stood there in silence. I was taking in what the doctor had said. Pops was fighting for his life. We could see him in the morning. And we'd be there when he found out he had lost his leg.

It was better than losing Pops.

The leg amputation was the bad news.

The good news was he was fighting. Pops was alive. They were confident he was going to make it. That was what mattered most.

.

THIRTY-FOUR – DECISIONS

June 21

The morning couldn't come fast enough. We weren't allowed at the recovery tent until seven AM. That's what we were told.

I couldn't sleep. I kept thinking of Pops and hoped he knew we were there waiting, and he wasn't alone. I thought of my mom, George, and Ruby. I wondered if they were searching for us, trying to reach as well.

I kept going on social media over and over.

A couple people actually liked my post and responded that they were glad I was okay.

It wasn't my mom or George, though.

Then I just started looking up people I knew. Some posted; some hadn't. I looked and found Sam the counselor from camp.

He hadn't updated.

Perhaps only those posting and checking were looking for someone or trying to get a message across. I didn't see any stupid post about politics or cats.

Then, on a whim, trying to pass time, I looked for Clark Westin. Surely, a man who apparently was off the grid wouldn't be on social media.

Sure, enough he was. Not only did he have an active "prepper" advice page, he had posted several times over the last two days.

Posts that people were reading and liking like crazy; even

commenting. Following him like he was this guru who was going to lead them all from the ashes of Yellowstone.

What should I do, Clark?
Do I put a mask on my dog?
I'm in Virginia. How bad do you think it will get?

Clark was in Kansas City and reporting how things were there. How he was in a school gymnasium with about two hundred other people waiting for his destination.

The gym was one of many places they were putting displaced refugees from the west.

I sent him a friend request, then commented on his recent post. I wasn't even sure he'd see it.

This is Marty. You met me and my brother. We are in Teetersville. Message me. Can you help me find my parents?

I didn't think he'd see it since it was buried in seventy or so comments.

About thirty minutes later, he accepted my request and sent me a private message.

"Good to hear from you," he wrote. "I'm glad you made it to safety. I take it your parents had evacuated by the time you got back home?"

I replied. "Yes. From the note that was left for us, they stated they were forced to evacuate."

"I worried that would be the case. That's why I asked for a picture of your mom."

"I can send it to you," I told him. "I can't get a hold of them. Their phones are off. I need them to know where we are and that we're supposed to leave on July second for Austin. Will you help?"

He wrote he would be happy to try. He had a few days, and they hadn't moved anyone out yet. It would happen soon. He'd look around and stated it shouldn't be hard because they registered everyone that had a space to lay their head.

I thanked him, gave him the names, forwarded pictures, and didn't mention anything about Pops getting hurt. I wanted to keep the information focused on my parents.

Ben thought it was good thinking on my part to do that. Even though we both knew how hard it would be for Clark. Finding them would be like searching for a needle in a haystack.

Finally, it was seven in the morning, and Ben and I anxiously waited outside the huge medical tent, which took up nearly a block. It was at the end of all the other buildings, trailers, and tents.

But we couldn't go inside. They stopped us. Others went in; but not us.

They asked our names and said someone would be out for us.

That frightened me. I kept thinking they weren't letting us in because something happened with Pops. It was already half past seven. We had stood out there so long that Clark had gotten back to me. He had checked four shelters. Nothing yet. He had a couple more to go. He'd find them if they were there.

They had to be there. Where else would they be?

It was so cold out, even with the canned fire. The snow was falling hard, and I shivered. Maybe it was only nerves.

We weren't there long before that woman, Rose, and her husband Ron showed up.

I found it odd and asked what they were doing here.

"We just wanted to talk to your grandfather. We heard he was awake," Rose said.

"Well, you have to wait until we talk to him," I snapped.

"Marty," Ben said my name softly, like a warning. "Be nice."

"She's fine," Rose said. "We understand. We will wait."

The doctor from the day before came out.

Doctor Carnahan approached us. "Wow," he said. "Mr. McCullen is popular."

"What's wrong?" slipped from my mouth as soon as I saw him. "Is something wrong with Pops?"

"Nothing is wrong with your grandfather." He shook his head. "He's doing very well. He's been up a couple hours. There was something that needed to be handled. I wanted you two to be aware he hasn't been told his leg was amputated."

"How does he not know?" I asked.

"He probably still feels it. And other things were going on.

We'll get to that. Just know this will be a big thing for you two to face with him. I just wanted to make sure you were ready."

I nodded.

"The healing will take a while. We don't have physical therapists. Not here nor do we have prosthetics. This will be a tough journey for him. Physically, he'll heal fast. The rest…" Carnahan shrugged. "I don't know. Come on in."

We stepped inside the huge tent. I looked over my shoulder, giving Rose a warning look to stay back.

Inside the tent, it was warm and dimly lit.

There were so many people in there on beds. The beds were narrow, a hybrid of a cot and bed. The patients lay there, lined up, alone.

Most had bandages and casts. It looked like a war zone from a movie.

We followed the doctor, barely squeezing down the aisle before we turned to the left.

I tried to be respectful and not bump into a cot.

"All these people," I said.

"Most are from a massive pile up on Eighty a couple days ago," Carnahan said. "Cars traveling in a government-mandated exodus. A fuel truck couldn't stop." He shook his head. "It was bad. Really bad. We were set up pretty quickly, so a lot came here."

He led us to the side, and I saw Pops laying on the bed. Ben and I rushed to him.

"You are a popular guy," said Carnahan. "People are waiting to talk to you. How are you feeling?"

"Oh Pops." I hugged him. "I'm so glad you're okay."

"I'm better," Pops said. "Now that I know these two are here and fine."

I laid my head against his shoulder, holding on to him. I could see the tube coming out of his chest and the blood-like contents flowing into a bag.

"Mr. McCullen," the doctor said. "You know you had some serious issues. We stopped the internal bleeding from the lung.

You should bounce back from that in less than a week. But the leg was bad. It was very bad. Though the kids did their best to set it, the ash caused it to get infected. And I… I am sorry. We had to take it."

Pops looked at him, then Ben, to me, then back to the doctor. "Where?"

"I'm… I'm sorry," the doctor said confused. "What do you mean, where?"

"You said you took it."

The doctor was taken aback, then kind of smiled awkwardly. "You're joking."

"I am. Look… I get it, I do," Pops said. "It's a serious thing to face. Ben…" Pops glanced at him. "Can you lift the blanket so I can get a look?"

The doctor waved out his hand. "It's a shock, Mr. McCullen. Just be prepared."

Ben didn't feel comfortable doing that, I could see it on his face. In fact, he lifted the blanket and didn't even look. As if we'd see something from a horror movie. Pops' leg was bandaged.

"Wow. It *is* gone," Pops said. Then, he sighed out heavily, "Guess I won't have to worry about those varicose veins anymore."

I stepped forward and pulled back the cover. "I'm sorry this happened, Pops."

"It's fine. All joking aside, I'm okay with this. Choice seemed pretty clear. Live without a leg or die with one. Unless…" He shifted his eyes to the doctor. "Unless I wasn't going to die."

"No, sir. You would have died."

"Good choice. Just know, I'll learn to live with this and make it work. Won't be anything I can't do with one leg that I did with two."

A clearing of a throat preceded the appearance of the government man, Aaron Siebert.

"Does that including handling your ranch?" Aaron asked. "I'm Aaron Siebert, sir. I'm in charge of agricultural emergency transport."

"The ranch business," Pops said.

"Yes. I have the final paperwork here. Your new land locations; government provisions you'll receive for doing this. Transport of you and the animals to your new location is July second." He looked at the doctor. "Will he be well enough to travel?"

"Yes," the doctor replied. "That's almost two weeks away. He'll be fine."

"Good." Aaron smiled. "But I am inclined to tell you, Mr. McCullen. If you choose to pass on the opportunity of the ranch, we can arrange for you to be on a senior ship, which is medical and rehabilitation."

"Like a floating nursing home?" Pops asked.

"Something like that, yes," Aaron said.

"Why would I do that?" Pops asked.

"Just realistically, you know working a ranch and running the livestock is hard work. Sunup to sundown. Hard enough with two legs, let alone one leg all by yourself."

Ben spoke up. "He won't be alone. We'll be with him. Me and my sister."

"And your parents?" Aaron asked.

I answered. "We don't know where they are. And instead of us transporting to find them or wandering around, it's better to stay put so they can find us. And when they do, all the more people to work."

Aaron nodded. "Okay. That works. I'll come back to finalize the paperwork. Maybe meet with your grandkids to go over some things."

"Question." Pops lifted his hand. "If I had decided on this nursing home on a boat, what would happen to my animals?"

"We'd divide them up. Actually…" Aaron turned and looked back, waving his hand. "Someone has offered already to take them."

Rose stepped from behind the curtain. "Hi, Bruce. Do you remember me?"

"I do," Pops said. "You're the one that got Bud Wheeler's stock for thirty percent going rate." Pops whistled. "You got a steal."

I murmured. "Sounds to me like she's trying to get a steal on yours now, too."

"Sounds like it," Pops said. "Thank you, but no thank you, Rose. My grandchildren will be handling a lot of the work."

Rose chuckled nervously. "They're children."

Aaron, again, cleared his throat. "They're teenagers. And I was working my grandfather's ranch at twelve. All day. Every day. Gotta start somewhere in this business."

I smiled at Aaron. "Thank you, Mr. Siebert."

The doctor lifted both his hands. "So, I have never had a patient get into a deep business discussion so soon after major surgery. I need him to rest. So… let him do that. All of you can visit later."

Rose did not seem happy. In a huff, she turned and walked out.

I kissed Pops on the cheek. "I'll be back after lunch."

"I'll expect you. Marty, can you go ahead? I want to talk to Ben."

"Sure."

After Aaron told Pops good luck, I walked out with him.

"Mr. Siebert, why would Rose get so upset about not getting extra work?"

"Because she's not getting extra animals," Aaron replied. "Think of this as a new government job. Ranchers and farmers are the future of America. They'll keep us fed. In return, we keep them going. The more you have, the more you do, the more you get."

I nodded. Still really not understanding.

Aaron gave a swat to my shoulder. "I'll be talking to you."

He seemed really nice and honest. I watched him walk away. I looked back at Ben and Pops. They were talking. I wondered what he was saying to Ben that he couldn't say to me. Probably some man stuff they thought I couldn't handle. Apparently, whatever Pops told Ben, he couldn't handle either. Ben's head lowered and it looked like his whole body sunk into mud.

What was it?

He would tell me.

I decided to wait for Ben outside. I took a few steps through the crowded tent and stopped when I heard it.

A whispering man's voice, froggy and almost breathless. He sounded like he painfully struggled to eke out, "Marty."

Someone was calling my name?

I looked left to right.

Nothing.

I was probably hearing things. The lack of sleep could do that.

After looking back one more time, I turned. And before I could take a step, a hand reached up from a cot and grabbed onto my arm.

They held tight. The hand was covered in some sort of netting. His arm was bandaged. In fact, half his body was bandaged.

I reached down to remove the death grip he had on my arm when I saw him.

Even though half his face was bandaged, the other half was not.

My legs turned to jelly. My insides shook, and I lost the ability to breathe or think.

Standing there in shock, it took everything I had to gasp out the words, "Oh my God! George."

THIRTY-FIVE – UNEXPECTED

"George!" His name gushed from my mouth, and I turned so he could see me. "Oh my God! George!"

What had happened to him? Why was he hurt?

"Marty… Ben?" He struggled to talk. The bandages crossed over just above his lips, and it looked like he had abrasions or a burn on his chin.

"Ben. Are you asking about Ben?"

He nodded slightly

"He's here. He's fine. Pops is too," I said. "I have to tell Ben. Oh, no wonder Clark didn't find you guys. You're here." At that point, I started rambling excitedly. "I hope you get better, George. Please get better. Pops… Pops got hurt; but he's going to be okay. Like you." I looked over my shoulder, aiming my voice to my brother. "Ben." I tried not to yell too loudly. "Ben. They're here. They aren't in Kansas." I looked back at George. "Did you know Pops was here?"

George shook his head.

"I bet he doesn't know you're here. Oh, man; is he gonna be so happy. Then that Rose lady who got Mr. Wheeler's cows is gonna freak." I glanced back Ben's way. He was staring at me. I waved for him to come over.

"Marty…" his voice quivered.

"Do you need me to let you rest?"

He shook his head. "So happy to see… you."

"I'm happy to see you, too." I leaned over and kissed the unbandaged part of his face. "I love you, George. I'll be back right back." Pulling back, I heard a sob escape George. It made me feel really bad. I had never heard George cry. "It's okay. I'll be back. I want to talk to Ben. We're gonna go find Mom and Ruby."

As I stepped away George grabbed my arm. I placed my hand over his. He was probably so happy to see us he didn't want to let me out of his sight.

"It's okay, George." I smiled at him. And when I turned to walk away, Ben approached.

His face was red, his lips pouty.

"Oh, no. Ben, is something wrong with Pops?" I asked. "I'll go talk to him. Then I want to find Mom and Ruby. I bet they're so worried. Can you believe we've been here a day and didn't see them?"

"Marty." Ben stepped up to me to stop me. "You can't."

"I can't what?"

"You can't find Mom and Ruby." Ben pursed his lips as he paused. "They're gone. They're gone."

I shook my head. "Did they go to Kansas?"

"Marty," his voice cracked. "Look at George. Look at George."

I slowly looked at George.

Thump.

I not only felt my heart beat strong, I heard it.

"They're gone," Ben spoke, weepy. "There was an accident..."

Thump. Thump.

"They left the exodus caravan to come here and wait for us. Had they just kept going..."

Thump. Thump. Thump.

I suddenly heard my conversation with Doctor Carnahan in my head.

"All these people."

"Most are from a massive pile up on Eighty a couple days ago. Cars traveling in a government-mandated exodus. A fuel truck couldn't stop. It was bad. Really bad. We were set up pretty quickly, so a lot came here."

"Marty. Mom and Ruby were..."

I didn't hear him say it. I didn't want to hear my brother say "dead" or "killed".

I flew from that tent before I had to hear it.

Once I got outside, I ran; slipping and sliding in the snow and ice. I didn't care about the cold. I screamed and cried as I ran; coughing and choking between sobs and shrieks as the cold snapped at my lungs.

I ran until I was clear of the tented street and trailers. Two blocks away near a gas station. I stopped, leaned against the wall of a "pay as you go" phone store until I crumbled to the snow-covered sidewalk.

It couldn't be true. It wasn't fair. Oh my God. My baby sister. My mother.

How? How?

I didn't even get a chance to say goodbye. Ruby was asleep? Did she know I kissed her and whispered that I loved her? My mother was a quick embrace, with advice to have a good time.

This wasn't how it was supposed to happen.

A massive super volcano erupted, and my mother and sister died in a car accident.

It wasn't fair.

It wasn't fair to Ruby. She was so little and precious.

I felt the anguish build in my chest, travel to my throat, and all I could do was grunt out a scream.

"Marty." Ben stood before me. "Let's go back to Pops."

I shook my head. "I can't."

"Well, you can't stay on the street. Let's go."

"How are you so calm?" I asked.

"I'm not. Inside I'm tore up. A part of me knew," Ben said. "I felt something was wrong. When they didn't call; we couldn't reach them. I just felt it."

"I know you did."

"I don't know what else to say. We can't change what happened. We can only accept it. As much as it hurts, we plow through. And it hurts." He extended his hand. "Let's go talk to Pops."

I grabbed my brother's hand and stood.

<><><><>

One thousand three hundred and twenty-two pictures were on my phone. Over half of them were of Ruby. In fact, I had the phone so long, it was her whole life. I adored my baby sister and every time she did something funny or cute, I took a picture.

I needed to see her face and Mom's one more time before going in the hospital tent.

I had seen the pictures a hundred times; but suddenly they looked different. Just looking at them felt different.

The second I saw Pops again, I cried. He said nothing. Nor did he stop me from burying my sobs on his shoulder.

Doctor Carnahan had come in and asked if I wanted something to calm me.

Before I could answer, Pops did.

"No. Not right now. Maybe later to sleep. Right now... I need her to calm down on her own so we can talk."

I don't know how long I cried or how long Ben stood there watching.

My brother never showed emotions, it was hard from him. But I could tell by his eyes, it was killing him.

"This morning," Pops explained. "When I woke up. They gave me some juice and were figuring out what they were gonna try to feed me. A nurse came in. She saw my name and asked me if I had a family member named George. That's when she told me. Boy, was she glad, for his sake, that I was here."

Ben continued. "That's why they made us wait. Pops was getting information."

"I wanted you both to find out before you saw George," Pops said. "But George saw you. He loves you kids so much. Couldn't love you more if you were his own."

"Why did you tell Ben?" I asked. "Why did you make him stay and not me?"

"Marty," Ben said. "Pops wanted me to break it to you. It

would be the best way. It would have been the best way."

"Do we know what happened?" I questioned.

"As far as I know, they were in that massive accident on Eighty," Pops replied. "The nurse said that George told them they had turned around and were headed west toward here. Figuring, I guess, you were maybe coming here. I don't know. They ran right into the accident. George, he doesn't wear his seatbelt and was thrown. Your mom... Ruby..." Pops winced. His voice cracked. "They remained in the car."

"Do they know for sure?" I asked. "I mean, maybe they went to another hospital."

"I don't know," Pops said. "George... He saw some things. He told the nurse he's certain they are gone... He's been sedated for a day. He's a mess. Physically and emotionally."

I wiped my hand across my face. "I don't know how I'm gonna do this."

"You will," Pops said. "As hard as it is right now, you will do this. There has been a massive event. So many people lost loved ones. You know what? It sucks. The world isn't over. We're still here."

"My world is over."

"It feels like it, I know," Pops reached out and grabbed my hand. "But it's not. What would your mom say to you right now?"

I shrugged.

"Well, you work on that, then. Figure out what your mom would say."

"We'll get through this Marty," Ben said. "We will. I promise you. We will. We have each other."

"We all have each other," Pops added. "We're still a family. We're a family that's pretty beat up and feeling crushed, but we're luckier than a lot. Because we're still together."

I knew what Pops was doing. He was trying to shine some light in a really dark place.

It wasn't going to work. Not for me and not yet. Not for a long while. All I wanted was my mom and my sister.

To see them.
Hear them.
Touch them.

From the moment I left them for the camp, I couldn't wait to get back.

The eruption at Yellowstone started a journey for me and my brother. A dangerous one, but we held onto hope that we would make it through and make it home. Even if we ended up thousands of miles away; one day, no matter how long it took, we'd see my mom and sister again.

That was the plan. That was the fairy tale ending for us all.

Since we walked out of camp into the ash, nothing was easy.

It was one obstacle after another.

A long, hard, painful journey.

That journey came to an end.

Unfortunately, it wasn't a happy ending

THIRTY-SIX – END OF ONE

September 14 – Ranch McCullen

The transport was supposed to leave on July second. But it took two additional days to clear the snow and ice from the train tracks. The entire camp in Teetersville left that day.
Everyone.
Most, with the exception of a few trucks, were loaded on a train with so many cars that it looked like a mile long. I'm sure it wasn't.
Box cars loaded with supplies, livestock. There was a medical car for those like George who still needed medical attention.
He would be transferred to a hospital in Austin. George suffered third-degree burns on thirty percent of his body. That wasn't from being thrown. It was when he went back to the highway and tried to get to the car to get my mother and sister but couldn't get beyond the flames from the tanker.
I can't image what he saw and heard. And I don't ever want to know.
George carries that with him. It would be up to us to help pull him through. He did say, because he never really saw them that last time, he was going to go back one day and see.
Maybe I'll go with him for closure. If there is any.
Pops was on a fierce fast mend. He wasn't letting anything get him down. He was out of the medical tent a full week before we left. It was hard to get him to rest and keep still.

At least he sat still on the train.

I once saw a movie where people were on a nonstop train through a frozen wasteland. I thought of that movie a lot as we plowed through the white and frozen landscape. It should have been beautiful and green. Instead, it was gray and cold.

Until we got farther south, and it wasn't as snowy. By the time we reached Texas, I could feel the temperature in the train warm up.

It took two days to unload the train cars and another three days to get everyone to where they needed to be.

Mass confusion, chaos, and fights. So many people and animals.

We kept to ourselves.

Finally, we were given the land and transported there. They called it Plot Nine, which Pops quickly changed to Ranch McCullen.

I knew he was disappointed when we arrived.

It was a small piece of land, with a barn, a modular home that looked like it was just dropped there, and a fence that was barely put together.

Once we got there and got our minimal things inside, Pops wasted no time putting Ben to work.

George finally came home on the first day of August. He still needed surgery and was always in pain. He made the difference in getting the new ranch together as best as he could. Fences were finished; feeding troughs built. We needed the extra help, especially since the government kept bringing us animals and expanding our land plot.

The weather stayed mild through the summer, which helped.

It was a lot of work and far from over. It would get cold before long, and we had to prepare for that.

I envied my brother Ben. He was so focused and strong. I knew he was still grieving our mom and sister, as I was. But I didn't handle it.

I cried a lot, hating the world at times.

Wishing I never went to that camp.

Pops was our anchor.

Without him, I don't know what I would do.

Physically, he was great. He had mastered the crutches, and said he'd eventually think about getting that prosthetic leg. The trauma of everything caused bouts of dementia to happen about once a week. Nothing severe. He'd forget George was hurt and that Mom and Ruby had died. Things like that.

I never corrected him because he never remembered saying things.

George told me that it would eventually get worse. I didn't want to think about that.

I wouldn't think about that until I had to. Hopefully, that would be for a long time.

Whatever happened with Pops, I knew I would never leave his side. Never give up on him.

He never gave up on us.

It had only been three months since the eruption happened, and the world went dark and cold. Technology was hanging on by a thread. The internet was out for most of the country, as was power.

We had daily rolling blackouts. No power at night. I made sure I kept my phone charged, even though we had no cell service. I didn't want to lose those pictures.

We were told eventually things would get better and back to where they were.

How was that even possible? Sure, the lights could come on for good. We could chat on our cell phones and post on social media. But it would never get back to where it was.

So many lives lost, and so many lives were changed.

Too much could never be replaced or gotten back.

The hurt would get easier but never go away.

At least I had my brother, Pops, and George. I embraced that thought every chance I got and whenever I was down.

That was more family than others had.

Like Pops said, we were a family. One that was beat up and

crushed; but we were still together.

And together, as a family, we'd forge through this new world we lived in.

It would be hard, but we'd make it.

I was certain.

[The End]

<><><><>

Thank you so much for diving into this book. I hope you enjoyed it.

Please visit my website www.jacquelinedruga.com and sign up for my mailing list for updates, freebies, new releases and giveaways. And, don't forget my new Kindle club!

Your support is invaluable to me. I welcome and respond to your feedback. Please feel free to email me at Jacqueline@jacquelinedruga.com

BOOKS BY THIS AUTHOR

Three Days After Impact

When the news of an impending extinction level meteor impact is made public, humanity struggles to find some way to survive.

Violet journals her life in a notebook in the form of letters to her grandmother. They start out sarcastic and funny, as she shares entertaining and exaggerated tales of her teenage life. But when Violet finds out about the meteor, everything changes. Suddenly she is thrust into a grown up world and her survival isn't guaranteed.

The pages of her journal are a journey. They detail the frightening and heartbreaking global catastrophe as it unfolds before her eyes.

The Black

Before the sun rose over the town of Sisterville everything went black. A natural disaster of unknown origins takes the lives of every living creature and decimates the small town.

Disgraced NASA scientist and now Cleveland Weatherman, Hero Galanis knows he is more than a local celebrity on television. He recognizes the anomaly on the satellite image as a repeat of the event that cost him his career. Decades earlier, Hero made predictions about the devastation the anomaly would cause, but those predictions pale in comparison to the reality the world currently faces.

The mysterious events are no longer popping up years apart, but now hours apart with no signs of slowing down. Nature is cleaning house and the reset button has been pressed. The extinction clock is ticking and mankind races to beat it.

The Black is a standalone novel.

We Who Remain

Just as the plane breaks the early morning sky, in a blink of an eye, 144 passengers onboard flight 6520 die.

There is no rhyme or reason.

Experts scramble to find an explanation on how and why those on Flight 6520 met their demise so quickly and violently.
It is hurriedly explained as a terror attack to the public, but General Buford Cane knows better. He has spent his entire career dedicated to the investigation and prevention of global threatening events. Behind the scenes, authorities are baffled as to what has happened and against the General's warning, they soon dismiss it as an isolated phenomenon.
He knows there is more.

The plane, the death of the passengers, are a prelude to something much bigger.

An event is on the horizon. An anomaly that can and will wipe out every single living being from the face of the earth.
Extinction is imminent unless something is done.

Printed in Great Britain
by Amazon